Stop Being
Frustrated
&
Overcharged
Year After Year By Your Workers' Compensation Program

52 ways to dramatically reduce your premiums,
eliminate overcharges and headaches,
and free yourself to focus on
growing and running your business!

by

David R Leng, CPCU, CIC, CBWA, CWCA, CRM

Publisher: Steve White, Norwell, MA

© 2014 by David R. Leng
All rights reserved.
No part of this book may be reproduced, scanned, or distributed in any printed or electronic form without the permission of the copyright owner. Requests for permission or further information should be addressed to David R. Leng, Duncan Financial Group, 311 Main St, Irwin, PA 15642

This book contains information about workers' compensation insurance and coverage. The information is not intended as a substitute for insurance, legal, or financial advice from an appropriately qualified professional and should not be treated as such. You should consult an appropriately qualified professional if you have any specific questions about any workers' compensation matters.

First Edition: April 2014
Printed in the United States of America
ISBN: [979-8630171191}

DEDICATION

To my loving wife and my wonderful children, the people I cherish the most, I would like to thank you for inspiring and putting up with me for the two and a half years it took to compile the data and write this book.

I would also like to dedicate this book to my late father, Ralph Leng, who could not see the book's final version. My dad always encouraged me to learn more in my professional career and guided me in that education. He always believed that the more knowledge you have, the better you can advise and take care of your clients.

INTRODUCTION

Dear Reader,

Today's technology has both overshadowed and enhanced much of yesterday's craftsmanship.

Now, most of us would definitely not compare a risk manager or an insurance professional to the craftsman who constructed our home or designed that jaw-dropping structure that makes us say "wow."

However, author David Leng aptly ties together a direct correlation between the risk manager and insurance professional to a craftsman. As a business owner, you will see and understand the uniqueness with which David works with his business clients. You will understand how he "builds a fortress" designed to fend off a multitude of employee injuries, view his varying techniques in which to help you appreciate varying Workers' Compensation insurance plans and how insurance companies think about you, then crush and ultimately control your Workers' Compensation insurance costs.

The Institute of WorkComp Professionals has trained many skilled and passionate insurance professionals. With this book, David Leng shows employers how he combines that skill and passion in creating a textbook approach to creating a Workers' Compensation program that actually *benefits* your business.

February 18, 2014

Preston L Diamond
Managing Director
Institute of WorkComp Professionals
Asheville, NC

TABLE OF CONTENTS

Preface		1
Chapter 1	How Can We Reduce Our Premiums?	3
Chapter 2	Why Do I Always Seem to Pay More Than I Expected for My Workers' Compensation Insurance?	11
Chapter 3	Why Does My Premium Go Up After a Claim (even when I paid more to the insurance company in premium than they paid for my claim?)	29
Chapter 4	Why do general contractors, property owners, and purchasers use our experience modifier to qualify or disqualify us?	47
Chapter 5	Why Is It That the Doctor the Insurance Company Recommends Sends My Injured Employees Home?	53
Chapter 6	Why Do Insurance Companies Charge Us for Subcontractors?	61
Chapter 7	We are OSHA compliant, so why do I have to pay for an injury to an employee that does something stupid?	71
Chapter 8	Why Do I Have To Pay A Claim On A Pre-existing Injury?	81
Chapter 9	How Do I Choose the Best Agent and Insurance Company to Insure My Business?	95
Chapter 10	What Is The Best Way To Get The Lowest Rates?	105
Chapter 11	Are There Better Ways To Insure My Business?	123

Appendixes **141**

Appendix A – Premium Audit Checklist to confirm you are not overpaying 142

Appendix B – Answers to Get Before You Hire a Broker 144

Appendix C – Items to be Reviewed as Part of Risk Management and HR Assessment 146

Acknowledgments **147**

About the Author **148**

Reader Bonus **150**

PREFACE

Over my 25-plus years as an Outsourced Risk Manager, many business owners, business leaders, and executives have expressed their frustration over the amount of time, energy and/or money they have spent dealing with their workers' compensation program without ever truly achieving the results they were looking for.

You can have some comfort in knowing that you are not alone if you are looking at the amount of money you have wasted on your workers' compensation program while wishing you could have used that money to accomplish a specific goal elsewhere in your business. Like many others, you may be similarly drained of the energy that is spent dealing with such issues as problematic employees and believing that this energy could have been better served to bring about a better outcome for you and your business. You also may share the feeling that your biggest regret is the amount of time frittered away trying to improve your workers' compensation program, only to fall short of the results you wanted and to now realize this time could have been better spent focusing on growing and running your business.

Whether you have 25 or 500 employees, as an owner or leader of a business, you likely wear multiple hats. Whether it is the management, finance, operations, human resources, safety, supervisor/foreman, risk management or claims management hat, wearing more than one hat is not an easy task. Most likely, one of those hats fits you more comfortably than the others. However, wearing multiple hats requires a balancing act, and almost all business owners and leaders have stated to me at one time or another that there is no perfect balance in wearing all of them successfully. And therein lies the problem.

All of these particular hats, or disciplines, are needed to grow and run your business, and will ultimately affect you in achieving the success you want in your workers' compensation program. They all need to be working together, utilizing the synergies that exist between them, in order to achieve that success. And if you lose focus of even one of them, you will most likely have reduced results or even significant problems with your workers' compensation program.

As a fellow business owner, the reason I wrote this book is that time after time we have been able to demonstrate how workers' compensation is actually controllable, much like most other areas of your business. When managed correctly, a well performing workers' compensation program can not only provide greater profits to your business, but also enable you to be more competitive in your marketplace.

This book cannot magically make your workers' compensation program successful. However, it *can* help you know more and accomplish more by giving you more tools and a better understanding of what can and should be achieved in reaching your workers' compensation goals. And in doing so, you will be able to concentrate and focus more on successfully growing and running your business.

———

How Can We Reduce Our Premiums?

This was the core question asked by the 1,187 owners, executives, supervisors, foremen, HR professionals, and accountants I met over a two year period, whether it was in a face-to-face meeting or speaking at a workshop. It did not matter if their business was insured using traditional insurance, such as a guaranteed cost program (which is what most business owners purchase), a dividend program, or a high deductible, self-insurance or captive alternative financing program. It did not matter if they were an owner or an employee. They all had the same basic question: "How can we reduce our workers' compensation costs?"

I have heard this question asked by more business leaders over the 25 plus years of my career as an Outsourced Risk Manager than I can count. Many of them thought achieving significant premium reductions to be on par with finding the Holy Grail, a quest often begun without actually knowing where to begin.

Initially, these business leaders focused on lowering their premiums, without fully understanding all of the complexities and costs that impact their workers' compensation program. And as a result they were unable to reduce their workers' compensation premiums. It is like reading the last chapter of a book first and then believing you understand everything that came before it. There are no short cuts. When it comes to workers' compensation, only by focusing on the entire book, on all of the cost drivers, will you, and they, be able to lower premiums.

I have successfully helped countless companies dramatically reduce their workers' compensation costs by having my clients focus all of their cost drivers and improving their *Risk Profile*. And in doing so, they have seen their premium reductions average 23% in just one year to 52% over five years.

You, too, can achieve similar results.

After meeting and talking to these business leaders, I came to the conclusion that they could be separated into two groups when it came to their state of mind with how they felt towards workers' compensation:

In the first group, a significant number were overwhelmed or lost. They were throwing their hands up in disgust believing that things were so bad there was nothing they could do to improve their outcome. They did not even know where to begin, or how to try to correct the situation they were already in. Their workers' compensation coverage was "killing" them from a profitability standpoint and taking away funds that could be used elsewhere to help grow their business. Equally important, working on the problems surrounding their workers' compensation program was draining the energy they needed to focus on successfully growing and running their business.

In the second group, the executives had a specific incident or two that had "driven them nuts," or cost them more money than they thought it should. It may have been a specific injury that went "big and ugly," or an employee that "milked the system" or "took them to the cleaners," as several owners have commented to me. It may have been an audit so large they were mystified as to why their business or employees were classified in a certain way. With these incidents, it was the proverbial "trying to close the barn door after the horses got out." They had gone too far down the path with nothing to do other than to try to hopefully outlast and somehow make it through a mucky situation. Fortunately, in many circumstances we were able to remedy the situation to a point where there was little or even no financial impact. Unfortunately, in other circumstances, there was no way to actually "fix" the situation and were still going to have deal with significantly larger premium costs as a result. In those situations, the best solution we could offer was to try and eliminate some headaches and frustrations and implement some corrective actions that potentially reduced some of the financial impact caused by their issues.

In either group, when the business leaders were overwhelmed they typically turned to the insurance marketplace, found some agents, attempted to get some quotes, and, if they were lucky, were able to obtain some minor relief for a year. One owner commented that he was "hoping to hit the lottery with huge premium savings" by shopping his insurance, but ultimately acknowledged he "wasted too much time, money and effort buying lottery tickets with nothing to show for it". In other words, he came to the conclusion that he would have been far better off focusing on solving his problems instead of wishing they would be solved for him. Ultimately, it did not appear that any of these business leaders were able to solve their problems, and none of them were truly happy with the results after they received their quotes.

The one sure fact is that bidding and quoting does not result in lowering your workers' compensation net cost, because….

- Bidding and quoting does not reduce your experience modifier, which is a large driver of your premium.

- Bidding and quoting will never enable you to reach your lowest experience modifier possible.

- Bidding and quoting has never validated whether or not your experience modifier is correct.

- Bidding and quoting has never prevented an employee injury.

- Bidding and quoting has never stopped an injured worker from visiting a medical provider who ends up putting them on medical leave.

- Bidding and quoting has never helped an injured worker return to work.

- Bidding and quoting has never stopped a workers' compensation attorney from getting into your wallet by inflating both the injury costs *and* your premium.

- Bidding and quoting has never prevented an insurance company from overcharging you for your workers' compensation coverage.

- Bidding and quoting has never guaranteed your employees are classified correctly on your workers' compensation policy.

- Bidding and quoting has never stopped your premium audit from being incorrect and resulting in overcharges.

- Bidding and quoting has never taught your employees the process for reporting injuries immediately, letting them know there will be no consequences, and that they will not have to pay any money out of their pocket for their care.

- Bidding and quoting has never stopped a fraudulent or exaggerated injury from costing you more money.

- Bidding and quoting has never stopped you from hiring an accident waiting to happen.

- Bidding and quoting has never helped create a Zero Accident Culture throughout your organization.

- Bidding and quoting has never stopped you from hiring a problematic employee.

- Bidding and quoting has never improved your *Risk Profile* – what an underwriter perceives the risk of your business to be and how they determine how much they want to charge you in premiums to insure your risks. In fact, bidding and quoting, if not done correctly, can actually create a negative risk profile or a negative appeal to insurance companies, which dramatically increases what they would provide in terms of insurance premiums.

I received questions about this from those 1,187 individuals and whittled them down to ten root questions that fairly well encompassed their concerns. I then put these questions into two different groups: tactical or strategic.

Tactical –
These are processes employers should do, or need to accomplish more effectively. For example, I have heard employers say, "we have a Return-to-Work Program, and return all of our injured employees to work as quickly as possible." But after conducting an injured worker cost analysis, we would find that 60% to 70% of the workers' compensation injury (claim) costs were from wages (indemnity), while the industry average shows that 40% of claim costs are from wages.

I have also heard employers say, "We are a very safe business," or "We are OSHA compliant." However, when we conduct an injury analysis and compare OSHA records and DART rates, we discovered that employees were suffering injuries 1.5 to 2.5 times more frequently than the number of injuries from comparable employers. It is possible to see from a quick analysis that the number of injuries, compared to the number of employees they have (frequency), revealed that 10% or more of their employees were hurt in any given year, which is a staggering amount no matter how you look at it.

Keep in mind high frequency will lead to more scrutiny from underwriters, and some underwriters look at frequency more than the costs of claims as a bigger reason to quote or not quote a business.

Strategic –
The other area of questions is strategic. This is where the rubber meets the road. There are certain concepts you need to understand and focus on to truly achieve better results for your organization.

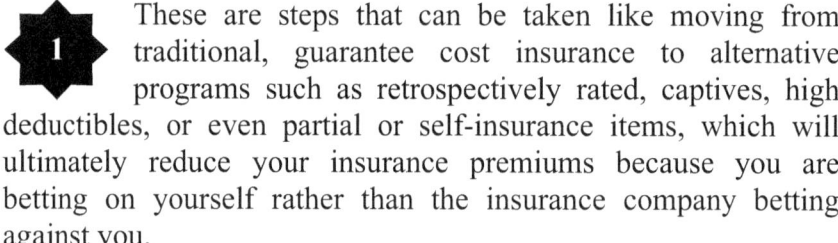

These are steps that can be taken like moving from traditional, guarantee cost insurance to alternative programs such as retrospectively rated, captives, high deductibles, or even partial or self-insurance items, which will ultimately reduce your insurance premiums because you are betting on yourself rather than the insurance company betting against you.

But keep in mind, rating programs cannot solve your problems. Many times insurance companies say, "We are going to put you on a retro (retrospectively rated program)" or, "We are going to put you on a high deductible program." However, they are not necessarily looking to reduce your premium, but to increase your exposure so that if you do not have the proper controls in place, the rating program they provided for you will enable them to collect more of your money and reduce their exposure.

You also need to focus on understanding *Risk Profile Improvement*. As I mentioned before, insurance companies base your premium on what they perceive your risk to be. I created the following premium formula to help you visualize how an underwriter looks at your business in order to calculate your Risk Profile and to determine the premium they will charge to insure you as a risk:

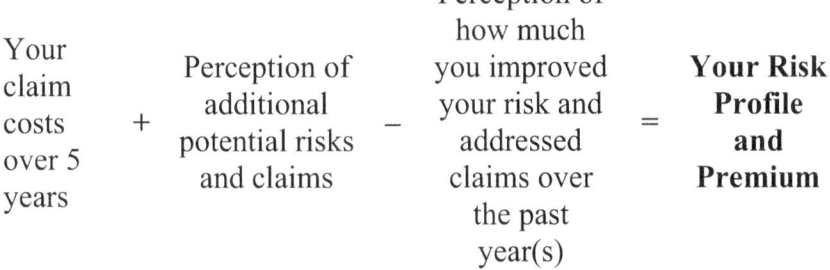

 Ultimately, the goal is to improve your *Risk Profile* by addressing some or all of the risks causing you to have higher premiums.

Now that you understand that bidding and quoting will not solve your problems, let us focus on what *is* in your control when it comes to workers' compensation. You need to learn how to overcome what your data (loss runs) shows, improve your Risk Profile, and truly make yourself more attractive to the insurance companies. By doing so, you can create a feeding frenzy in the marketplace leading to significant reductions in your insurance costs.

Let us focus now on questions executives and professionals have expressed over the past two years. We will cover several areas: understanding the financing of injuries and policy program management; understanding the management of injuries; understanding how to prevent injuries; understanding true risk management or Risk Profile Improvement; understanding risk transfer; and understanding how to best engage with agents and insurance companies.

Why Do I Always Seem to Pay More Than I Expected for My Workers' Compensation Insurance?

This question is asked by almost every executive I meet. Why do they end up paying more for their workers' compensation policy than they anticipated? This is especially true when the subject of their year-end policy payroll audit is discussed.

The root of the question revolves around "tactical" issues, including your year-end policy payroll audit, the classifications that you should have on your policy, and the credits that you should or could have applied to your policy. It is necessary to provide some overview as to what you need to do to maintain better control of your premium.

First is the premium audit.

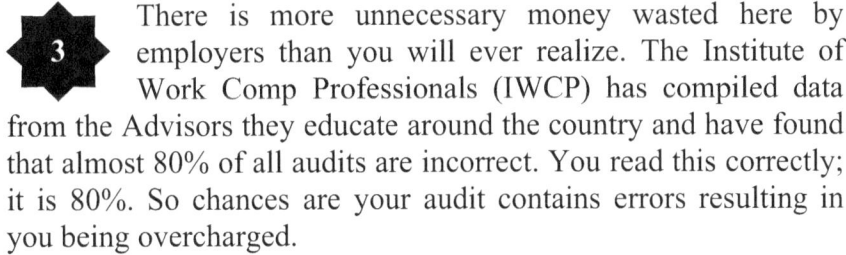

There is more unnecessary money wasted here by employers than you will ever realize. The Institute of Work Comp Professionals (IWCP) has compiled data from the Advisors they educate around the country and have found that almost 80% of all audits are incorrect. You read this correctly; it is 80%. So chances are your audit contains errors resulting in you being overcharged.

The Institute has recently reported that a certified Advisor found a $404,000 error paid by an employer because of mistakes made during the audit. The employer had changed the business from a manufacturing operation to that of a wholesaler by means of outsourcing all manufacturing. The insurance company or agent, not recognizing that this organization evolved into a different type of business that needed different classifications (and lower rates), dropped the ball, resulting in a $404,000 overcharge.

Fortunately, the Advisor identified this significant oversight, made the changes with the insurance company, and was able to recover the money. But not before the employer had lost two years' use of that capital that could have been utilized to improve their business during the recent economic recession.

In another instance, we corrected and recovered a $381,480 error for an executive who came to us complaining about his premium. In this case, the auditor misapplied rules relating to the Voluntary Workers' Compensation endorsement which the business had on their policy.

These two examples are extreme in the amounts returned to the business owners, but errors of hundreds, thousands and even tens of thousands, are quite common. Therefore, it is important that you make certain your premium audit is error free.

The issues with audits are related to how the audit is conducted. Typically, the auditor, as well as the employer, is motivated to get the audit process over as quickly as possible. Auditors are good, hardworking people who typically are working with less than all the information that they really need. Still, they would not be disappointed if the audit generated an additional premium for the insurance company. Therein lies the problem.

Keep in mind auditors are the eyes and ears of the insurance company, whether they are an independent auditor or insurance company employee. They are there to determine the final rating basis (payroll) for your policy, and to understand what business you are in and determine if you are properly classified.

Most people do not realize auditors typically report to the insurance company finance department, and not the underwriting department. After the auditor determines the final payroll audit, the payroll totals go through the accounting department, where they are calculated into the final audited premium and you get a bill for the difference.

This is why most businesses typically receive the final audit bill first, and then at some point later they receive the report showing what payroll totals were used in the audit. Which leads us to the question, "Why am I paying so much and why do these payrolls appear to be incorrect?"

Let us start by understanding how the payroll audit process works, or in other words, the map the auditor follows as a checklist to reduce the likelihood they miss something. The auditor asks for your quarterly unemployment tax filings, your payroll records, your ledger, and your financials so they can also verify your payrolls and see who you use as a subcontractor.

Once they have that information, they take your entire payroll amount and place it into the class code with the highest rate on your policy. This class code is commonly referred to as your "governing class code," where everyone ends up who does not fully fit into any of your other available class codes with lower rates. Then they ask you, "Okay, who works in the office?", "Who works in sales?", as these class codes typically have much lower rates than your highest rate governing class code.

If you happen to forget anybody in that process, these employees end up going into your highest rated class code. You need to make certain that the person working with the auditor knows exactly who your employees are, where they work, and what they do. This way, your employees do not end up inadvertently misclassified. You do not want your clerical person being rated in a higher rate class code and you being overcharged.

For example, I met a roofing business' controller who was in attendance at their industry association's workers' compensation workshop in which I was the keynote speaker. After providing an overview of the audit process, much like we just went through in this chapter, I noticed that she was looking rather uncomfortable, so I asked her, "What's wrong?" She said that their premium audit was conducted the previous week and the auditor was in and out in about 10-15 minutes, and she was worried.

She said the auditor requested their payroll reports, quarterly unemployment tax reports and ledger. He then asked if there was anything else she had prepared for him. She did not know what exactly he was asking for, so she did not have anything additional prepared. At that point, he looked everything over and said that if he had any questions he would give her a call. He never called again.

She called me about three weeks later and sent me their auditor worksheets I suggested she request from her insurance company. I found that all the people in the office, including her, were classified in the roofing classification at a rate of $32.89 per $100 of payroll. The office people should have been in the clerical office classification at a rate of $0.39 per $100, a dramatic difference.

To make it worse, the auditor included a charge for all the subcontractors used, even though the contractor did have certificates of insurance for all of them. The issue is, if copies of certificates of insurance are not provided as proof that the subcontractors maintained insurance, the auditor is allowed to charge for "uninsured" subcontractors. So he did without even bothering to ask for them.

We filed an audit dispute with the insurance company so the employer did not immediately have to pay the audit invoice. We then fixed the errors by compiling all of the necessary job descriptions of the employees and certificates of insurance of the subcontractors. The result was the employer did not have to pay $43,842 in overcharges. It was a success, but a complete headache and nuisance to the employer.

4 Please understand several things about your audit. You need to know what should and should not be included as payroll. It varies by state, but typically there are anywhere from 15 to 18 types of payroll that should not be included in the audit. These can be found in your state's workers' compensation manual under Excluded Remuneration.

5 For example, one of the Excluded Remunerations is employee fringe benefits. If an employee has a business car it is a taxable income charge which typically ends up on their W2 tax form, but it can be excluded from the payroll being used on the audit. Meal Money provided when employees work late should also be excluded. And in some states, expenses such as tool or uniform allowances can be excluded.

6 If you are a contractor that performs Davis-Bacon (prevailing wage) work, you may be able to deduct the fringe benefit portion of the wage payment to your employees. The rules vary by state as to the required documentation needed to be able to deduct the fringe benefit amount.

7 Also, there are minimum and maximum amounts that apply when calculating the chargeable wage for officers. Payroll for officers are capped, and any earnings over that capped amount are to be excluded in the audit. Reversely, if an officer does not take a payroll, or only a token amount, but works for the business, they are usually charged for a minimum amount of payroll as they are still covered for medical costs of an injury.

Another item that might be excluded is severance pay. If you pay an employee two weeks' severance upon

termination, or you have a situation where you want to offer a severance package to make an employee "go away quietly," this severance pay should not be included in your audit. Keep in mind though, that unused vacation time, PTO (Paid Time Off) days, and sick days which have been accumulated and are still owed to the employee, are included in the audit.

9 If you do not provide proof that your subcontractor has workers' compensation insurance, the insurance companies will charge for them. The reason is that most courts will rule that an uninsured subcontractor or individual or sole proprietor may be under your control and direction at the time of injury. The subcontractor will, therefore, be viewed as an employee and would be eligible for workers' compensation coverage. Hence, the insurance companies charge for uninsured subcontractors. This also applies to sole proprietors and owner operators that do not provide proof of workers' compensation coverage. More on subcontractors to follow in a later chapter.

It is best to have all of your certificates of insurance showing workers' compensation coverage ready and available for the auditor. If you do not have proof of coverage from your subcontractors, you should understand the rules the auditor follows for charging for uninsured subcontractors:

- If you hire a subcontractor who is providing you with only labor, most states will allow you to reduce the amount paid by 10% for audit purposes. This allowance is for the overhead and profit of the subcontractor as the entire amount you paid the subcontractor was not used as wages for their employees.

- If the subcontractor you hire is providing material and labor, the rules allow you to reduce the amount you paid by 50%. This allowance is for the cost of material versus the amount paid as wages to the subcontractor's employees. Some insurance companies may require you to go through significant effort by requesting all of the detailed invoicing from your subcontractors so they can pull the cost of materials out. Therefore, you should check your state's workers' compensation manual on how to determine this amount.

- Lastly, if you are hiring a subcontractor who operates mobile equipment, such as a crane or a truck for delivery, the auditor should reduce the amount paid to the subcontractor by two-thirds, knowing that most of that cost paid to them is going to paying for, maintaining, and fueling that equipment or truck.

So much money is involved in your audit that it is very important for you to understand the audit rules. Think of it this way… would you go to an IRS audit without all of your bases covered and an expert at your side? Well, then why would you go to your workers' compensation audit without being similarly protected?

An IRS audit is rare, whereas a workers' compensation audit is annual. You need to be equally prepared. The audit rules are the rules, however, there are some gray areas you can push on if you have a defensible position. However, keep in mind that you absolutely do not want to commit fraud.

10 The problem is that agents, insurance companies, and the auditors are not educating their clients on how to properly prepare for an audit. Prior to the auditor's arrival, you should prepare the complete audit and not just provide the auditor with the information. You want to have the complete audit finalized, with all the data formatted and totaled, so you know what the outcome will be *before* the auditor arrives. Eliminate surprises.

You want to build yourself an overcharge-proof audit package. You want to utilize spreadsheets or templates and make sure you classify each employee into the correct classification. You want to provide, show, and justify the excluded payroll or excluded remuneration. You want to have a summary statement ready so that you know what your payroll totals should be. But most of all make certain that all of your totals balance to match your payroll records. Because if they do not match, the auditor will conduct the audit their way, and most likely you will not like the outcome.

Appendix A of this book includes a list of questions you may want to ask yourself to gage if you may have been overcharged on your audit. If you have, it still may not be too late to seek to recover any overcharges.

 You can download a FREE COPY of our AuditCheck Program™ manual from www.PremiumReductionCenter.com/audit. Because of its size, it is very difficult to include within these pages the entire packet we provide to our clients to assist them in obtaining an error-free audit.

Second, we can dig into classifications.

 There are over 600 classifications. Keep in mind bureau rules classify a business as a whole (although there are exceptions) by what you do, what you sell, what you make, or how you make it. As we discussed previously, the "governing class code" assigned to your business is the default classification that best fits your business as the bureau will not provide individual classifications based on each and every function your employees conduct

 The exceptions to this are construction and staffing, where you can classify an employee based on what specific task they do, assuming you keep the appropriate payroll and time records for each task.

If you track, for example, time worked for an employee working as a carpenter for one hour, the next hour a plumber, the next hour a roofer, and the next hour a drywall installer, you can actually apply the wages for each hour to each classification. If you do not keep such records, the auditor then will classify that employee by the highest rated task performed and do so for the entire year. It is best that you make sure you are tracking wages earned by each classification by the hour, or at least by the job, so that you are not charged higher rates for the whole year.

Also, keep in mind that in some states the insurance company is allowed to change your classification at the time of the audit. The auditor is never allowed to change or add a classification if the new classification would have a higher rate associated with it. They could only do so if the insurance company endorsed the policy prior to the end of the policy year that they are going to be auditing. They can only change or add classifications to lower rates, not raise them.

Given the number of classifications, please understand what your business is and what classifications apply to you. There are many nuances you need to understand, so having an expert on your side is financially critical.

An example of this can be seen with an electrical contractor. Sounds like a simple class, however, there are classification codes based on inside work, outside work, and high voltage work. Then within inside work, there is a separate classification if a business installs Cat5 wire, coaxial or fiber-optic wire. This separate classification code for low voltage inside work is usually buried in the "fine print" of the Burglar Alarm Installation classification code.

You need to look at fine details of all the classifications available to you, but be warned. Before you request a change of classification, the first rule of thumb is always "**Do No Harm!**"

> For example, I was once contacted by an employer to help him get control of his workers' compensation costs. One of the things he said was that an agent commented that his business should be classified as a "*precision* machine shop" instead of a "machine shop." A precision machine shop is an eligible class code for a machine shop that has more

than 50% of its work completed for customers is required to be within 0.001 of an inch tolerance or better. The classification code change would have an excellent result for the owner as the precision machine shop rate is almost 40% lower than the machine shop rate.

While touring the facility, I developed a clear understanding of how they made their parts, and felt they were a well-run operation. However, they were more than just a precision machine shop. After the tour concluded, I asked the owner if the agent went through his facility. With a puzzled look on his face, he said he could not remember taking the agent through the shop.

When I asked him if the request for the classification inspection audit from the bureau (bureau inspection is required by that state to make any classification changes) was already made, he said the bureau was coming the next day. I suggested he cancel that inspection.

The reason for my concern was that the business had an aluminum smelting area. Basically, the employees would take worn out parts, add liquid aluminum to them, and once cooled, they could then machine the parts to the customer's tight specifications.

My fear was if the bureau came to conduct their classification audit they would classify this employer as a smelting operation, much like a foundry, because of their employees working with molten metal.

Unfortunately, the employer could not cancel the classification audit. I attended the audit and discovered my initial assessment was correct. The auditor was going to classify them as a smelting operation. The smelting classification code rate was more than double that of the machine shop rate he currently had, and even worse, the smelting rate was almost four times the rate of the precision machine shop rate he was hoping to receive. However, after the auditor stated he would be changing the classification to smelting, I was able to run my idea past the auditor of having the business owner put in a full wall that would provide a clearly defined physical working area for the smelting operation that separated it from the rest of the facility. In addition to the physical barrier, I was looking to suggest to the employer that he change his operations slightly so there was one dedicated employee who would perform all of the required aluminum pouring, rather than all employees.

By suggesting these changes, my goal was to have the auditor agree that only one employee (or possibly two employees if the bureau auditor would have asked who backs up the one individual when he is out) would be classified at the much higher smelting rate and hopefully receive the approval of precision machine shop for the rest of the operation and shop employees.

The auditor agreed with these changes and we scheduled a secondary follow-up meeting three weeks later after the wall was to be completed.

In the end, the owner was happy to be informed that the auditor agreed that since it was only one employee out of 34 who was exposed to the more hazardous work of aluminum pouring and the other employees were physically separated and protected from that operation, all shop employees would be classified as precision machine shop.

Make certain that you will receive a lower rate classification, and not a higher rate classification, when you request any change to your class codes.

There are many other classifications that are commonly misapplied. If you are a sheet metal contractor, there are classifications for inside shop sheet metal as well as some for outside sheet metal work, with two different rates.

For paving contractors, there are separate classifications for street and road construction, street and road sub-surface work, and for parking lots and driveways. Each of these three classifications has different rates.

Some states have a separate class code for employees whose primary job is to drive delivery vehicles, even if delivering your own goods or materials. Others states do not separate drivers out as a separate class code and therefore include drivers in the governing class code of the business.

You need to investigate exactly what you do and what classification should truly apply. Sometimes just changing where somebody physically works, or how they do something, can make a difference in their classification.

Important Note:
In addition to the classification, you also must be aware that if you are an employer working upon or near a navigable body of water, you may also need to carry Longshoremen and Harbor Workers (USL&H) coverage which is a different rate and classification than you normally would have.

This is also true if you have an employee working as a crew of a boat on a navigable body of water. Such employees are subject to the Jones Act, and special coverage would need to be purchased to provide the coverage needed to meet the Act's requirements.

> For example, a concrete construction contractor was going to drill to obtain core samples in a levy wall along a river. These samples needed to be drilled on the water side of the wall, and therefore the contractor needed to rent a barge to work from. A barge business placed the barge where the work was to be performed and the contractor hired a boat and pilot to shuttle the employees from a wharf to the

barge. In this example, the employees would be subject to the USL&H coverage, but not the Jones Act as they were not the crew of the boat. On the other hand, if the contractor had rented or owned the shuttle boat and piloted it themselves, or rented and placed the barge themselves, then there would be employees subject to the Jones Act and the contractor would be required to have Jones Act coverage. Either way, you should consult a professional before you conduct any work on or near a navigable body of water.

Third, are rating program credits.

There are a number of credits programs available to employers that offer premium reductions for participating in these programs. At last count, 36 states and the District of Columbia offer programs that can reduce your premiums. Not all states offer the same programs, and each state varies in how they are implemented. Therefore you should research what programs are available to your business in your state(s). I will highlight the most common ones:

Safety Programs

Typically you will need to form a committee comprising general employees and management. The committee will need to maintain proof of meetings with written agendas, minutes and attendance records. Members will need to be trained on safety specific to your operations, conduct inspections of your facilities, and conduct post-accident investigations and recommend corrective actions to prevent incidents from reoccurring. In many cases, external training and inspection (auditing) of the committee is required to receive the program credits.

Using the Risk Profile formula presented to you in the introduction, you can impact the *Perception of how much you improved your risk and addressed claims over the past year(s)* by managing a proactive and effective safety committee. You can use the committee and their notes to highlight and offer proof of the changes you have made to your organization to improve your Risk Profile.

Drug and Alcohol Free Workplace Programs

Unfortunately, just stating that you have a drug-free workplace or having your employees pledge to that affect is not enough. Typically you will need to meet the following requirements:

- Have and distribute a written drug-free workplace policy
- Conduct employee and supervisory training
- Establish a policy to include, and conduct testing for the following situations: pre-employment, random, post-accident, and reasonable suspicion testing;
- Establish protocols if an employee fails, and retesting if need be
- Establish an employee assistance program (EAP)

Please remember that state and federal laws must be followed in the administration of your drug-free workplace program, and laws do vary by state.

Managed Care Programs

You can receive a discount if you use an approved third-party managed care provider. The thought behind this program is that proper injury management in a cost containment (pre-negotiated reduced fees) by specifically trained medical personnel familiar with work related injuries will result in lower medical costs and hopefully faster recovery and therefore lower wage (indemnity) costs.

More on managing medical costs in Chapter 5.

Construction Classification Premium Adjustment Programs

Some contractors may pay their employees a much higher wage per hour in comparison to their peers, particularly those involved in Davis-Bacon, prevailing wage jobs. There are a number of states that offer a premium adjustment program to avoid penalizing these employers for their higher wages.

Credits are determined based on your average hourly payroll, including overtime and bonuses. The greater the average hourly wage you pay to your construction employees over the minimum hourly rate required by your state's program, the higher the credit you will receive. The amount can be as great as 40% in some states.

To qualify for the program, you must first be able to prove the average hourly wage for all your construction employees (even part-time workers) is greater than the required minimum amount. You will have to submit your payroll and hour records each year to receive the credit. Typically, you will be using your payroll and hours from your third quarter payroll data.

Deductible Programs

You can receive a credit for taking a deductible for each claim that occurs. Deductibles can vary starting at small amounts of $1,000 or $5,000, and go to large amounts of $50,000, $100,000, $250,000 or greater. Obviously, the higher the deductible, the larger the credit that you would receive.

More on deductible programs in Chapter 11.

Schedule Rating Programs

Most states allow insurance company underwriters to vary the premium that they can charge you for your operations through the use of Schedule Rating. These are subjective credits or debits (surcharges) used by an underwriter based on their perception of your *Risk Profile*. They are based upon your risk control management experience, safety program, hiring practices, etc. Typically, the maximum credit or surcharge an underwriter can apply is 25%. In order to assist underwriters, the Pennsylvania Compensation Rating Bureau even goes so far as to offer a suggested Risk Characteristic Chart in Pennsylvania's state workers' compensation manual. They identified the following risk characteristics for assignment of credits or debits subject to the maximum ranges of 25%:

Features of Workplace Maintenance or Operation	-10% to +10%
Risk Elements Not Addressed in Classification Plan	-10% to +10%
Availability of Medical Facilities in or Near Workplace	-5% to +5%
Safety Equipment/Devices Present in/Missing From Workplace	-5% to +5%
Extraordinary Safety Programs Applicable to Workplace	-5% to +5%
Qualifications of Employees	-10% to +10%
Accommodations/Cooperation with Carrier by Management	-5% to +5%
Considerations Related to Policy Expenses	-5% to +5%
Other Risk Characteristics Not Addressed Above (Specify)	-10% to +10

The Pennsylvania Manual goes on to state "Schedule rating adjustments for any given risk shall be based on information contained in the carrier's files and records when the credit or debit is determined, and such supporting information must be retained in the carrier's files and records for such risk throughout the period of time in which the policy is subject to audit under provisions of the policy."

In other words, the underwriter must have documentation as to why they are applying credits or surcharges to your policy. This is where your *Risk Profile* can have a significant impact on your premium, good or bad. As the credit or surcharge is subjective, it is important for you to provide documentation that the underwriter can clearly see and use to justify why and how much they are using as credits on your policy.

More on understanding and impacting your Risk Profile and rates in Chapter 10.

Why Does My Premium Go Up After a Claim?
(even when I paid more to the insurance company in premium than they paid for my claim)

The increasing of premiums, particularly following claims, is a frequent frustration voiced by executives. The issue is that most executives do not truly understand what their experience modifier is, how it works, how it is calculated, or even if it is correct.

Because employers tend to focus solely on their workers' compensation premium, almost all executives overlook the experience modification factor and its link to creating a competitive advantage in the marketplace. Although workers' compensation is certainly a significant and costly employee benefit, it also is a powerful business benchmark that can tell you how well your business is operating.

20 The experience modifier is the biggest driver of a business' workers' compensation premium. The lower your experience modifier is the lower your premium will be. Therefore, companies with lower modifiers have a lower production cost structure. This lower cost structure leads to being more competitive, which leads to securing more jobs and more profitability. The exact opposite is true as well. A higher modifier leads to higher costs and makes it is more difficult to compete for work.

My goal is for you to better understand your experience modifier, how it is calculated, what it costs, and how it impacts your organization.

Research by the Institute of WorkComp Professionals (IWCP) finds that 10-15% of modifiers are incorrect, and almost all of them are mismanaged. **This means you are most likely being overcharged.**

> For example, the owner of a 55-employee fiber optic cable line installer had a 1.65 experience modifier, due to a large number of employee injuries. The owner, who is classified into the first group mentioned in Chapter 1, was overwhelmed and frustrated by his workers' compensation program, in part because he was not getting the correct answers or advice from his agent. He was struggling to pay a premium of almost $200,000 in the assigned (high) risk insurance pool and was in danger of being put out of business.
>
> When we first talked, he asked if I could direct him to an insurance company that might be able to save him money. It seems another agent had just provided him with a quote that would save him about $20,000 and was pressuring him to accept it. Although the quote was interesting, it was not enough to really take the financial pressure off of him.
>
> Because he felt under pressure from the time requirements needed to accept the agents quote, I asked him if he could give us two weeks to dig in and understand more about why his modifier was so high and what was causing his claims and premium increases, before talking once again with the agent. He agreed.
>
> We gathered all his loss information, and obtained a copy of the experience modifier worksheet. We also asked for his past audited payrolls, which allowed us to determine that the bad news was going to get worse as his experience

modifier was going to go from 1.65 to 2.04 the following year and he was facing a premium of $250,000, even with the current quote from the agent. This was obviously *not* the news he was hoping to hear.

The other interesting thing was, if he accepted the quote and changed his policy midyear it would have caused his worst claims' year to linger on his experience modifier for a fourth year instead of the normal three years. We actually determined that moving his policy to this early date would cost him over $40,000 more in premium because of the claim impacting the experience modifier for that extra year.

It was apparent that the agent did not understand the rules surrounding the calculation of experience modifiers. Rating bureaus do not like policy date changes as it alters the basis of the data used. Although typically based on a three-year period, experience modifiers can be based on up to 45 months (three years and nine months) of your historical experience, so you have to be certain a bad claim or a bad year does not linger on your experience modifier longer than it needs to or it will cost you money.

The good news is that after taking the time to analyze the experience modifier and the losses, we actually determined that three of the claims were related. The insurance company had reported that only *two* of them were related, and they were capped together as one catastrophe claim. Unfortunately, this business had two employees injured in the same accident, one critically. These are the two the insurance company reported as a catastrophe. However, as the accident was unfolding, another employee rushed to try and prevent the incident from occurring, but in doing so this Good Samaritan fell and injured his knee.

We believed that this third injury would never have occurred if it were not for the initial incident, and was therefore a strong causal link.

We petitioned the insurance company to make a correction by filing with the bureau to have all three injuries linked as one catastrophe. They took the position that it was a separate claim as the employee was injured in a fall and not by the same event as the other two employees.

We then appealed to the state bureau who, fortunately, agreed with us. Because of this, we were able to get the injury reclassified as being part of the same catastrophe claim. The recalculation took the business owner's experience modifiers of 1.29, 1.65 and the projected 2.04 for his next anniversary date (renewal), to a revised 1.02, 1.28 and a projection of 1.53, respectively.

What this meant was the employer actually received a check for the current and previous years of $86,000 due to the retroactive recalculation. The insurance company had to correct his experience modifier for current and previous policy years and refund him the difference in premium. Plus, this business owner would see a reduction in premium for the coming policy term as a result of now having the correct lower experience modifier.

We also overhauled their safety program, their return-to-work program, and installed a more robust program to improve their risk profile. We were able to make the business look more attractive to underwriters by impacting the *"Perception of how much you improved your risk and addressed claims over the past year(s)"* portion of the risk profile and premium formula. We were also able to get an insurance company to remove this employer from the assigned risk program. The new program ultimately saved the employer more than $100,000.

So in a short three-month span, we were able to fill this client's pocket with over $200,000 by uncovering errors in their experience modifier and improving their risk profile.

Your experience modifier is based on your data, claim dollars and payroll amounts over a three year period, not including your most recent completed policy year. This data gets reported to the bureau, which compares it to other companies in the same classification. For instance, if you are a carpentry contractor, your losses in relation to your payroll amount is compared, in proportion, to other carpenters as a whole.

If your losses meet expectations, you earn an average grade, which is a 1.00 experience modifier. If you are above average, you receive a credit modifier (ex. 0.91), and if you are below average you receive a surcharged modifier (ex. 1.26).

To put it another way, if you were in school and just met expectations, you would receive an average grade of C. If your child came home with a C, would you be happy?

But this is an actuarial formula. Unfortunately, most insurance agents will come to you and say: "Hey! You have a 0.94 experience modifier. That is great! You are getting a credit of 6% for a great loss history." However, is that really a good comparison when your minimum experience modifier could be 0.61?

Think of it this way, if your experience modifier is 0.94, and your minimum is 0.61, you are really paying 54% more for your workers' compensation than you are legally obligated to pay because you are paying more than what your minimum modifier is.

To put the actuarial experience modifier in easier terms, all you need to really know is that for every dollar that the insurance company pays for an injury, or expects to pay, adds points to your experience modifier. Every point that gets added to your experience modifier increases your premium. Therefore, the effect of an experience modifier is that you will repay the cost of injuries, with interest, back to the insurance company over those three years.

Simply put, all the workers' compensation rating bureaus do is compile the information that the insurance companies provide them. They basically determine what classification codes are available and should be used by a business, determine what the rate for each classification code should be, and calculate each business' experience modifier. If the bureau calculating your experience modifier receives bad data the bureau will spit out bad data, resulting in an incorrect experience modifier.

Ask yourself: Do you know what the most important date of your workers' compensation coverage is? Most employers initially answer this as their renewal date, which is when they see what they are paying in premium for the year.

In reality, the most important date is what we call the "Kodak Moment," the date your data goes to the rating bureau. That date is six months following the expiration date of your policy. The mid-policy year, when you are most likely not thinking about your insurance, is actually when you should be worried the most. You need to make certain that the information going out to the bureau is correct.

21 You also need to understand claim reserves – the amount that the insurance company must legally set aside for what they predict the future injury cost to be – counts just as much as if it were actually paid when it comes to calculating your modifier.

So if for some reason, something occurs during the process where an employee may be recovering faster than expected, it would be reasonable for the insurance company to reduce the amount of reserves. But if they do not reduce the reserve before that date, it is etched in stone and you are going to be overcharged. It is important that you pay attention, not only when you are looking at your insurance for possible quoting purposes but also before your experience modifier is actually calculated.

To give you an example, I met with the owner and the CFO of a chain of automobile dealerships about two months prior to their renewal. They went on and on about how great their insurance company was, how often they visited and provided loss control services, how they handled their claims, and even highlighted that the insurance company met with them quarterly to review their claims and adjusted the reserves downwards for them. I was actually beginning to question why they had invited me to meet with them about reducing their workers' compensation costs; I would normally hear complaints from a business that was dealing with a whopping 1.58 experience modifier.

They handed me the information from their mid-year claim review, which was held just shy of a month prior to their mid-year valuation date. The loss runs, with detailed claim descriptions, were marked all over with the CFO's handwritten notes. The CFO noted several claims in which the insurance company agreed to take a closer look at the reserves. They also handed me the loss runs and their experience modifier worksheet for their upcoming renewal, which they had received the day before during their pre-renewal claim review. The most recent loss runs had several claims marked with highlighter, accompanied by a note from the claims representative stating that the reserves of the highlighted claims were reduced. The executives bragged about how well the insurance company was doing for them.

I quickly compared their experience modifier worksheet to the loss runs they just received, as well as those they received at the pre-valuation date mid-year review. What I found both shocked and angered the owner and CFO. Despite meeting with the executives prior to the valuation date and agreeing to review the reserves, the insurance company reduced the reserves *after* their valuation date. The cost to their business was an additional $89,438 at their next renewal because of this.

We tried but it was too late to fix the problem. The insurance company denied agreeing to a certain dollar amount of reductions and would not recalculate the modifier. They stated it takes time to review the medical files of specific claims, which is necessary when setting or adjusting reserves.

When appealing to the rating bureau, the bureau employee stated that the employer did not have the hard documentation proving the insurance company agreed to specific reserve changes prior to the valuation date. Therefore, the bureau would not make any corrections. The bureau employee further stated that reserve changes throughout the year are very common, changes made after the valuation date are not a clerical error, and therefore the bureau would be unable to correct the modifier.

This example indicates how critical it is to stay on top of your claim reserves and to make sure that they are accurate. Reserving is more of an art than a science, so some variance is to be expected. You just want to make certain that the reserves are in line with the direction and expected outcome of the claim.

On the subject of claims and reserves, I want to take a moment to address two terms that are very frequently used in discussions regarding claims. Both of these terms were used by the previously mentioned automobile dealership executives when we were digging into their specific injuries and their related claim costs. Unfortunately, the evolution of the use of these terms has led to some misconceptions as to how they should be used and the actual impact they have when an underwriter determines your risk profile and premium.

The first misconception is surrounding the term *"Shock Loss"*. While digging into the details of their claims, the two executives used the term "shock loss" when describing a certain injury. They used the term "shock loss" to mean this injury was a very large, unfortunate claim. They believed that since it was a "shock loss" that the impact of that claim on their premium should be minimized or fully eliminated. We will have more on this term to follow.

The second term that has a misconception was used by these executives as a reason that a claim should not count or fully count against them, stating "that employee does not work here anymore." The problem is they are addressing the wrong question, or issue. The reason that an underwriter is asking if the employee still works there is because it may be a situation where an underwriter is concerned that the employee will be reinjured. For example, does the employee have a claim or two for a strained back, a torn rotator cuff, or something to that affect? Is a specific employee an injury repeater who has had three or four injuries? Certainly in these situations, an insurance company would want to know if the employee is still working for the employer and if there is likelihood that person will get reinjured.

> An extreme example of this was an excavation and paving contractor who believed his experience modifier, and therefore his premium, was higher than it should be. While digging into the nine injuries on his loss runs, he tried validating his point of being overcharged for his workers' compensation coverage by stating that three different claims were "shock losses", and that the "injured employee no longer works here" for the four of the remaining six claims.

> One of the "shock losses" was a near fatality. An employee who was spreading gravel over a water collection pipe of a drainage system next to the foundation of a house was injured when the six foot deep trench he was working in collapsed. This collapse resulted from the contractor not placing a trench box into the trench to protect his worker from the ground collapsing, nor did he properly grade the slope of the trench so it could not collapse. This was a clear OSHA violation. The injured employee was

frantically rescued by coworkers, but not before being crushed by the collapsing ground and ending up in the hospital for 2 ½ months. Now, eight years later, he is still barely able to walk.

The contractor believed he should be absolved of most or the entire fault for the injury to this employee, as well as from six others of his nine injured employees. He believed that almost all of the injuries were just "bad luck," and "not his fault," and therefore should not count against him. But this was not a single, isolated injury he was concerned about, but injuries to most of his employees. So clearly this was more than just a case of "bad luck".

The contractor was in complete denial that he was ultimately responsible for how he hired, trained and protected his employees. He refused to believe that most of the severe injuries to his employees could have been avoided had he taken the steps to properly supervise, train and protect his workers. He was in denial that underwriters could see through the improper use of these terms, and when it came to the *"Perception of additional potential risks and claims,"* underwriters wanted to charge him more premium due to what they believed the future claims could be.

As a further comment on Risk Profile and an underwriter's *"Perception of additional potential risks and claims"*, one underwriter commented to me that four of the injured employees were no longer working for the contractor, which clearly demonstrated how poorly he managed his employees. The underwriter even went so far as to make the case that the employer's return-to-work program, which he claimed to be a focus of his business, really did not work. In other words, underwriters do not believe just what you say to them, they need to see proof to back it up.

> This contractor is not alone in his denial. I recently met with a manufacturing business who was non-renewed due to losses and was not happy with their new insurance company when their premium went from $189,343 to

$519,115. It is important to note that my initial meeting occurred less than one month after they had to accept that policy with the dramatic increase in premium. They were looking for me to help them find insurance companies to quote their workers' compensation insurance despite the fact that they had several large brokers that had just tried to provide them with quotes. Bidding through four insurance agencies had resulted in a 174% increase – almost 2 ¾ times what they used to be paying.

I point this out as another example because on the loss runs they handed me, I saw "no longer working here" noted next to 6 of their 10 largest claims, and 23 of 104 injuries that occurred over the last five years. Only one of the six larger claims was from an employee who has had multiple claims while working there, which is why an insurance company wants to know if they were still employed there. This business was averaging over 20 injuries a year, and with around 200 employees, that means over 10% of their employees were being injured in any given year: a staggering amount. Clearly this employer was in denial that they needed to improve their safety and return-to –work programs. And it is another reason that bidding and quoting will not solve your problems.

The reason I am pointing out these misconceptions is that "shock loss" and "the employee no longer works here" have been so frequently misused in the insurance industry that it seems that once either term is used in describing an injury that there is a belief by business leaders that no further discussion is needed and that the impact of such claims should be minimized when an underwriter calculated their premium. The examples of how these terms are being used clearly points out the false beliefs that these concepts have created.

How did these misconceptions come about? Let's face it, discussing large, costly claims and their effects on your premium can have a very emotional affect on business leaders, and not a positive one. This is especially true if the employer believes their business was "taken advantage of". Many agents, and even insurance company personnel, will state it was a "shock loss" or tell you not to worry about it as "the employee no longer works for you" in an effort to make you feel better and end a heated or uncomfortable discussion. In other words, they tell you what you want to hear, not what you need to hear.

You really cannot excuse any claim away, because to an insurance company there is really no such thing as a "shock loss." For example, you have a salesperson stopped at a red light on the way to an appointment and someone comes through the intersection and slams into them, causing your employee to become paralyzed. It really is not your employee's fault, but statistically speaking auto accidents occur and, therefore, auto accidents are contemplated in the salesperson's rate. That is why the salesperson classification has a higher rate than the clerical office classification. So the insurance company is not going to fully dismiss it because it was not your fault – "it is out there." Remember, workers' compensation is "No Fault" insurance. It pays even when it was not your fault an employee is injured.

In this example, the insurance company could subrogate, or seek to recover the money they spent on the claim of the paralyzed employee, which would result in a lower amount, or no amount paid out. Receiving subrogation from the at-fault party will clearly reduce the impact the claim has on your premium. However, the reality is that in most situations, the amount that is recovered does not reimburse the insurance company for the total amount spent, leaving the amount paid for the injury to go against your experience modifier and loss ratio. Since most subrogation situations leave the insurance company short of a full recovery; underwriters will not fully dismiss such an incident when it comes to the pricing of your policy.

Continuing to use this example and the premium formula, if you have a sales force that travels, the underwriter's *"Perception of additional potential risks and claims"* is that eventually one of your sales people will be injured in an auto accident (whether at the fault of the salesperson or the other driver) so they will not discount an injury from a large not-at-fault accident. However, in this example, let us pretend that following this accident, you decide to cease having your own sales force and begin to use independent manufacturer representatives to sell your products. This change will impact the underwriter's *"Perception of how much you improved your risk and addressed claims over the past year(s)."* As you no longer have the ability to have a salesperson injured in the course of driving, the underwriter may discount the injury from the auto accident.

23 I have had many lengthy conversations with underwriters on this subject while discussing claims and negotiating premiums for our clients. Based on these conversations, the only time underwriters will truly and fully dismiss an injury is when the cause of an injury was eliminated or engineered away.

24 Another example would be if you had an employee who was severely injured while using an older production machine where the guarding was not up to standards or it required manual interaction by the employee. If you purchase a new state of the art, automated machine to replace it and therefore eliminate the dangerous one, the underwriter will be able to discount, or possibly dismiss the injury when it comes to determining how much premium they would want to charge you.

Tracking Success
Now that you understand you are repaying for any and all injuries, with interest, it is important to determine whether you are doing a good, fair or bad job. Are you improving or trending in the wrong direction? There are certain data points we suggest every executive analyze every year, so you can benchmark your progress. These can be complied into what we refer to as *Your Annual Executive Briefing*.

Your Annual Executive Briefing includes:

- *Your Minimum Experience Modifier* – How low can your experience modifier go? If you do not know this, how can you benchmark how much extra money your claims are costing you?

- *Your Controllable Experience Modifier* – The gap between your current experience modifier and your desired, minimum experience modifier.

- *Your Ultimate Cost of Loss, a.k.a. Your Payback Ratio* – For each dollar the insurance company spends for an injury, how much are you paying back to the insurance company for that injury over the three years that it impacts your experience modifier?

- *Your Actual Losses versus Expected Losses* – Are you doing better or worse than average? This report shows you a year by year comparison of how much your claim dollars are in comparison to what the rating bureau expected based on your reported payrolls.

Benchmark your results. If you do not measure it, you cannot determine if you are doing a good job or not. You must focus long term to earn an "A" on your modifier report card.

Think of an experience modifier like a hockey game. A hockey game consists of three periods; your experience modifier is based on three years. Your team can absolutely overwhelm the opposition for two periods by having two great years. But if in the third period, or the third year, the opposition comes out and crushes you – you can still lose. So if you have one bad period, or one bad year by taking your eye off the puck for one minute, it can cost you the game, or in this case, when the final buzzer rings it can cause you to have a surcharged experience modifier which costs you money.

Understanding you are repaying an injury with interest back to the insurance company, because of the calculation of your modifier, is a financial incentive to bring injured employees back to work. This reduces the cost of the claim, which is your goal. There is more on the subject of "Return to Work" in Chapter 5.

Unfortunately, your increase in premium from your modifier is only part of the problem. The medical and wage costs of the injury, and the resulting increase in premium are direct costs. In addition to direct costs, you experience indirect costs. Indirect cost estimates range from four to 10 times the cost that is actually paid out. Examples are: Lost productivity time, workforce disruption, having to pay overtime to cover that loss of production or missing employee, reduced morale, property damage to products, equipment or work; scheduled delays and unhappy customers. These are additional concerns that add to the cost beyond your workers' compensation payments to the injured employee, or the doctor's office, and they increase your overall workers' compensation costs.

A Pete Marwick study suggested how much more employers would have to produce to cover the injury costs of an employee. For an injury that costs $2,000, a soft drink bottler would have to bottle 244,000 cans of soda to cover that $2,000 loss; a baker would have to make 953,000 donuts. So every dollar paid for an injury is taking away from the profits of the jobs or the products you are putting into the marketplace. This is a great way to explain to your employees why not having injuries is important. With the information from Your Annual Executive Briefing, you can calculate how much a $2,000 injury will cost your business in comparable production.

After understanding your experience modifier in more detail, it is then common for you to ask, why did our premiums go up more than just what the modifier caused? Why is our insurance company using higher rates as well? In addition to the impact of the modifier, other things influence insurance company underwriters when they look to offering you a quote. They look at your *Risk Profile*, which we cover in detail in Chapter 10.

Here is a quick answer. Because of certain claims the underwriter may view you as a higher risk and increase your premium further. One of the things to remember is that when it comes to your actual premium, there are three components: Your payroll (audited each year… you could be overcharged); your $ rate per 100 of payroll that you get charged (we will explain later as to how you can impact that in Chapter 10); and your experience modifier.

Another area that is often overlooked is "subrogation." We will use the example again of the employee sitting in their car at the traffic light who is hit by another driver. We discussed how such an unlucky accident is contemplated in the rates. The costs of the employee's injuries also impact the calculation of your experience modifier, even though the accident was not your employee's fault. As we pointed out, the insurance company can go after the negligent driver and recover its money, or in other words, receive subrogation.

If done properly, even though it might take up to five years for the insurance company to recover funds from another party, subrogation should be reapplied to not only your current year's experience modifier, but also reapplied to all of the years that were affected by that claim, retroactively, and premiums returned to you.

So it is also important to make certain that your insurance company subrogates on your behalf and reports correctly so your experience modifier is recalculated retroactively. We have seen cases where the insurance company recovers its spent money and the employer does not see a dollar of it because it is lost in the insurance company's system and the modifier is never recalculated.

As you can now see, there are a multitude of reasons why your premium is more than you really expect. The good news is you can control all of the events with a knowledgeable insurance agent.

Why do general contractors, property owners and purchasers use our experience modifier to qualify or disqualify us?

We have already discussed the experience modifier as one of the biggest drivers of your workers' compensation costs. The lower the modifier, the lower the rates; therefore, companies with lower modifiers have lower productivity cost structures.

The lower cost structures lead to your business being more competitive and securing more jobs with more profitability. The exact opposite is true as well. Higher modifiers lead to higher costs and make it more difficult to compete for work.

Face it; in today's sluggish environment companies and risk managers are using the experience modifier as a significant determining factor to disqualify firms from bidding on projects. If your experience modifier is over 1.00, your business may be viewed as unsafe and therefore will be unlikely to get the job.

Companies know they need to do something about their modifier but do not know what to do. The good news is your modifier is just as manageable as any other business function as long as you are motivated to do so. Here are a couple of examples:

Example #1
        A machine shop with a 1.301 experience modifier six years ago has worked hard and smart to drive it down to 0.745, which is the third best out of 228 companies with that class

code in the state. Before implementing changes to improve their modifier they were unable to receive a multimillion dollar contract, even as the lowest bidder, because the purchasing business' risk manager viewed them as an unsafe business and questioned the quality of their work. They now have been able to win the contract and have grown from 58 to 110 employees.

Example #2

The 55-employee fiber optic line installer being crushed by their 1.65 experience modifier had their backs up against the wall when the telecommunications business they work for informed them they had just two years to attain compliance with their safety guidelines, including a requirement to have their experience modifier below 1.00. The concern was that the telecommunications business represented 90% of their work. Losing the contract would most likely mean shutting the doors as they also did not qualify for other companies' line of work because of their high experience modifier.

We were able to get the contractor an extension to four years to attain modifier compliance. However, the telecommunications business required the contractor to hit benchmarks in terms of number of injuries that would be verified through loss runs from their insurance company and their OSHA logs. Secondly, they had to initiate an aggressive behavior-based safety program to cut their frequency of injury by almost 60% to be compliant in the first year and 80% in two years.

Based on the results of the new safety programs, they were able to become compliant and actually went 19 months without an injury. They will be in compliance of the experience modifier below 1.00 within three years as well. They are expected to now be able to bid on other telecommunications work as well.

The reason why organizations use the experience modifier as a qualifier or disqualifier is because they are published by third parties, namely, the NCCI (The National Council on Compensation Insurance) or various state rating bureaus. They are therefore viewed as being correct or even as "audited results."

Whereas OSHA Frequency Rates or DART Rates (Days Away, Restricted and Transferred) may be more accurate in terms of a business being safe or unsafe, many organizations view the OSHA rates as flawed because they believe it is possible for an employer to "fudge" or manipulate the data.

It is critical for you to confirm that your experience modifier is correct, to find and fix errors, and to follow up with your insurance company by frequently seeking subrogation for your not-at-fault incidents caused by third parties.

We have seen companies whose experience modifier has gone above 1.00, not because they are an unsafe business or have too many claims, but because they are determined to keep their premium down to the lowest point each year. Sounds a bit confusing, so let me give you an example:

> I was once approached by a commercial building contractor because the insurance company had requested the rating bureau add roofing, which has a significantly high rate, to their available classification codes. He was looking for help to prevent this from occurring. This contractor, who was in the process of doing a number of roofs, said that the combination of the higher roofing rate was more than double his other classes, and his 1.388 experience modifier would cause him basically to go out of business because of the amount of premium he would have to pay.
>
> We determined they had actually been doing roofing jobs for a number of years, so the odds of stopping the roofing class from being added to their policy was definitely *not* in their favor. Therefore, if we could not stop the new

classification from being added, we did the next best thing by asking the rating bureau to have the experience modifier recalculated to take advantage of the higher expected losses. I had the contractor provide us with what his payrolls would have been over the period of the last four years with the roofing classification on his policy, and determined that his experience modifier instead of being 1.388 would be closer to 0.85.

By "artificially" having their payroll placed in their governing classification, which was a much lower rate in comparison to the roofing rate, the affect was the expected losses portion of the modifier equation was much lower than they should have been. Because of this, when the contractor did have some incidences, albeit minor, they were in essence magnified or exaggerated by the experience modifier calculation and his modifier rose well over 1.00.

Think of the modifier equation as a playground see-saw: your claims on one end and your expected losses on the other. By having the payroll placed in an incorrect and "lighter" rate classification, it made the expected losses "lighter" which had a negative affect causing the actual losses of the contractor to appear to be "heavier" or worse than they actually were and to go "out of balance" and end up over 1.00.

Fortunately, we were able to work with the state bureau and their insurance company to redo the past audits, without any additional premium owed for the past policies. We also asked the state to recalculate the experience modifier going forward. The modifier was recalculated to 0.844.

The result: the contractor went from actually getting thrown off a couple jobs because of his high experience modifier to receiving requests to take over the jobs of other dismissed contractors because of how low his experience modifier was. More importantly, the contractor went from putting money into his business to stay afloat while waiting out the problem of his experience modifier being over 1.00, to actually having one of his most profitable years ever.

But here is the most interesting thing of all. The premium that the contractor had to pay, even with the roofing classification added to the policy, was within $3,000 (2.4%) of what the contractor would have paid without the roofing classification code and the higher experience modifier. In other words, your premium is all about your claim costs, and your modifier will balance things out in the end.

26 When you have claims, your experience modifier and premium will eventually reflect that. Having payroll incorrectly assigned to a classification with lower rates in an effort to lower your premium for that year ultimately costs you because your experience modifier will eventually be incorrect and inflated – think see-saw again. Therefore, you will end up paying a higher premium anyway from the higher experience modifier, and could face the situation where you are disqualified from performing work for others due to that inflated modifier.

Once again, the idea is to make certain you are putting the appropriate payroll in each of the appropriate classifications for the audit, that you are being diligent that your modifier is correct, that you seek to correct the errors as quickly as possible, and that you make certain subrogation is occurring so your experience modifier can be corrected retroactively. But more importantly, you should focus on not having the injuries that end up on your modifier and minimize those that do through proper claims management.

Why Is It That the Doctor the Insurance Company Recommends Sends My Injured Employees Home?

Having a doctor that does not require an employee to return to work is very frustrating for employers who understand the value of an early return-to-work process. Let me give you a bit of background why some of these things may be occurring, and an understanding as to why injury costs are escalating.

The National Council of Compensation Insurance (NCCI) has been tracking workers' compensation costs for decades. There has been a significant change in how the costs line up. For example, in 1987, medical costs represented 46% of all injury costs, and indemnity (wages) payments were 54%.

Shift to 1997, just 10 years later, and medical costs were 53% compared to wages at 47%. In 2007, medical went up to a whopping 59% while wages reduced to 41%.

On the surface it could be viewed as companies doing a better job of returning employees to work. But in reality, the amount paid to employees out of work due to an injury is actually up. It is just that the amount spent on medical care is exploding. This is why health insurance premiums are also increasing.

Through all of this, the insurance companies and third-party administrators have been increasing their focus on reducing medical costs, particularly through the reduction of fees to doctors and facilities. The insurance companies even tout the "savings" to their clients as a way of showing where their medical cost containment programs have brought them.

Interestingly enough, at the 2012 NCCI conference in Orlando, Florida, the NCCI announced that these fee reductions have had little impact on curtailing medical costs. Focusing on the medical fees is really not the solution; you need to focus on having the injured employee receive the best treatment as quickly as possible. This includes both the quality of medical treatment the employee receives *and* how the employee is treated by your business.

You need to take charge of the process, because if you do not, you are leaving it to the whim of the doctor, the insurance company, perhaps even the employee himself as to when he is fit to return to work.

Business people often rely on the insurance company adjuster for input as to when to bring the employee back to work, decisions directing care, etc. This is the issue. Because insurance companies try to keep their expense costs as low as possible, many adjusters are servicing upwards of 250 or more claims at one time.

The "best" insurance companies' tout their average claims per adjuster are around 100 claims or less, which means they would have more time to focus on managing your claims as compared to an adjuster with over 250 claims would. However, if you ask them how many total claims the insurance company has, and how many trainee adjusters they have working on cases, you find that the seasoned adjusters are still probably handling 150 or more claims. The problem ends up being that your priority—which is your claim—may not necessarily be the priority of that adjuster. You must take control of the process yourself.

Ask yourself: Who are the three most impactful people when it comes to having a better outcome?

- The doctor.

    The doctor can understand that an employee being at work recovers quicker than one who is sitting at home. They can understand that not being sedentary is actually good for an employee's healing process. Plus, the loss of a significant social environment at work can weigh heavily on an employee's psyche. Or, they can send the injured employee home.

- The employer.

    The employer can be caring. They can bring the employee back to work. They can accommodate any variety of conditions and provide meaningful work, so that the employee feels he is still a valuable member of the team. Or, they can send the employee home.

- The employee.

    The employee can either be compliant or disruptive. They could follow the suggestions and recommendations of the doctors and try to recover as quickly as possible and return to work. Or, they can become disruptive. They could seek out an attorney. They could exaggerate how serious their condition is to the doctor in order to receive time off from work.

If you look at it, these are the three most important people and organizations that affect an outcome. You may notice the adjuster is missing from this group. Although the adjuster is important, they can only manage, and react, based on the decisions of the other three.

If the doctor says the employee is to be off work, all the adjuster can try to do is wait for the doctor to release the employee to full or modified duty, or order an independent medical evaluation and fight to bring the employee back sooner. If the employee wants to get an attorney, an adjuster really cannot stop it. When that occurs, they have to go into the mode of settling the claim as quickly as possible to reduce overall costs.

The Doctor

Clearly the doctor wields the pen and is critical in this process. You need to choose, and choose wisely. Some of the questions you need to ask yourself are:

- Are you relying on a doctor that the insurance company provided to you; one off of a discount provider list?

- Do you know who your doctor is when an employee suffers an injury?

- Do you know what experience the doctor has in treating workers' compensation injuries? Keep this in mind: many doctors seek to treat workers' compensation injuries because it is currently more lucrative from a fee schedule than healthcare. In the past, many doctors ran from it because it was less lucrative.

- What is your doctor's return-to-work philosophy?

- How will the doctor communicate with you and how often?

- What kind of wait times does the doctor have?

- What exactly are the doctor's capabilities? Are they able to remove metals from the eye, provide sutures, and take x-rays, for example? Or will you have to send the employee to an Emergency Room to get these services? Keep in mind when using an Emergency Room that the odds are the medical costs and chances of the employee being taken off work will be much higher.

- Did the doctor come and tour your facility to understand the requirements of the jobs?

- More importantly, does the doctor know what your capabilities are in terms of early return to work?

- Is the doctor related by ownership or contract with secondary facilities such as physical therapy or imaging facilities? In some cases, we have seen higher than average utilization of those facilities. It would not be unexpected for someone, who is looking to offset the fee reductions for each service to increase the overall number of services.

- Does the doctor follow ACOEM (American College of Occupational and Environmental Medicine) standards? Doctors who follow these standards are typically Occupational Medicine doctors who are specifically trained to deal with work-related injuries. By following the ACOEM standards, the doctor has best practices guidelines to follow for each type of injury rather than doing multiple tests that most likely have no bearing on the injury.

You need to create doctor relationships that will work best to bring the employee back to work and provide better employee care. This ultimately leads to better medical outcomes, which leads to less medical costs and far less wage or indemnity costs because the employee is back to work quicker and is ultimately happier in the end game.

The Employee
What I have found over time is there are basically two types of employees: good employees and bad employees. However, there are subsets. You have good employees who, no matter what, will always be good. They will come back to work and follow the doctor's instructions. They will never be a problem.

You can have bad employees that will remain bad, no matter how much you and the doctors try. To be honest, if you think you have a bad employee you are much better off getting them out of your organization before they become an injury or claim.

On rare occasions, you can have a bad employee that turns good. Usually, the employee will not turn good after they are injured, but it could happen before they are injured if you appropriately engage them in a corrective process. You can try to change their attitude or whatever the case may be. However, if you cannot turn them around you should probably eliminate them from your organization or, as my one of my friend says, "I am going to help them free up their future."

However, many times we see good employees who turn bad. When I talk to employers about a particular claim, especially a large claim, I hear many times the employer was surprised that this employee took advantage of them.

When drilling down on a claim, we usually find the employee sat at home for a while with no contact from the employer, other than maybe the HR person, and no contact from any of their coworkers. Much later, after the employee has been sitting there, the insurance company urges the employer to bring the employee back to work. The insurance company wants the employer to start putting pressure on the employee to return to work.

In some cases, the employee has shown up but often been handed meaningless work. When this happens, the employee may view this as harassment or that the job was given to them as a kind of punishment.

The key is to educate your injured employee on what to expect, and what you expect from them. You need to explain that you care, that you expect them to go to the doctor, that you expect them to follow the care plan, and that you want them to have a full recovery first and foremost. Also, explain they will need to return to work because they are a *valued member of your team*. Let them know that if they cannot do their original job, even with some alterations, that you have other key projects they can do that are less physical.

Continually reach out to that employee if they are away from work for more than one day. It might be a coworker, a supervisor, or even an executive. An injured employee should be everyone's concern, and everyone needs to engage with the employee on an ongoing basis in order to reinforce that you want them to get well quickly, that you miss them, and that you need them back on the team.

 Your strongest deterrent from an injured employee lawsuit is that **nobody sues someone they like**. Maintaining a good relationship with your employee is key.

The Employer
Demonstrate that you care. Statistics show that 70% of employees off of work did not hear from their supervisor, a coworker, or anybody other than the HR or Workers' Comp administrator from the time they were off to the time that they returned. How does this make your employee feel?

Second, you need to find meaningful work for the employee. Ask your managers or supervisors for unfinished projects that need completing. Ask them what they would like to get done if they had more time and more help. You can even create a temporary position such as Safety Monitor where you provide observation checklists for the employee to go through the facility or job site to determine if the employees are doing what they are supposed to be doing.

Most importantly, you do not want to pay the employee to sit at home. Yes, it saves you money from the Payback Ratio of your experience modifier, and it does make the insurance company somewhat happy that they are paying out less money, but it will not improve the outcome any more than if they were receiving compensation from your workers' compensation insurance company. I have seen many an injured employee paid to stay home, only to eventually wind up with a very big settlement check.

The overriding fact we see relating to the success of bringing an injured employee back to work is their relationship with their supervisor. If they have a good relationship with the supervisor prior to the injury, they typically will come back to work faster. However, if that relationship is suffering, it may be more difficult. It is critical for you to train your supervisors on the importance of why employees must follow the business' early return-to-work program.

A supervisor's relationship with your injured employees, and how the supervisor communicates, measures the success of your return-to-work program. Supervisors who communicate poorly, have a poor attitude, or do not care, will sink your return-to-work program.

Clearly, you need to provide meaningful work to your employee to get them back as quickly as possible. Make sure the doctor on your team will send them back to work. Even though 24% of injuries result in an employee off work for more than three days, statistics show that it should really only be 10%. The difference is a result of not having an active, successful return-to-work program, not having a doctor who understands your organization, and not communicating your expectations properly with your employee.

As we mentioned, currently 60% of injury costs come from medical costs and 40% from indemnity wages. I contend that by getting the injured employee the right care as quickly as possible, and controlling the wages more and getting the employee back to work as quickly as possible, you will actually reduce your overall medical costs. When an employee wants to stay off work, they have to find more and more reasons to go to the doctor to get permission to stay off work.

Why Do Insurance Companies Charge Us for Subcontractors?

The reason why insurance companies can and do charge for subcontractors is rather straight forward. It relates to the fact that there are either laws on the books, or case law, that deal with an injured person at a job site (or at a facility) who was injured in the course of doing the work they were contracted to do, and the duty owed, if any, to that person. The complication comes when the subcontractor is able to demonstrate that the organization which hired them had control over what they were doing at the time of injury, thus creating an employer-employee relationship.

Understanding how to properly address this issue is bigger than just your workers' compensation policy, and whether or not you are charged for an insured subcontractor. We will need to dig into how you hire subcontractors in general, what requirements you put on them, and as the word subcontractor implies, understand what need there is for a contract and contractual risk transfer.

Clearly, the easiest way to avoid the problem is to only hire organizations that have insurance and workers' compensation coverage. However, that is sometimes impossible or simply creates a significant headache whenever you need to hire somebody with a specific skill set or when it turns out the subcontractor does not have workers' compensation either through lapse or cancellation.

As an example as to why it is important for you to make sure that your subcontractors have workers' compensation coverage, we will go through the situation a home remodeler faced.

> The remodeler, who happened to be a franchise organization, needed to subcontract some exterior painting of a home. The remodeler hired a painter through a bid process and ended up hiring a particular subcontractor. When the bid was submitted the subcontractor provided a certificate of insurance with both general liability and workers' compensation coverage.
>
> The subcontractor, in addition to providing a certificate showing his insurance, also had his own business and location advertised in the phone book, advertised his business on the side of his own truck, had his own business card, and had his own tools of the trade such as ladders, rollers, and power-spray painters. Basically, he had all the tools necessary to do the job. He clearly worked for others and worked directly for homeowners.
>
> In this situation, you would have a solid case showing that this individual, who was hired to do the painting, really was his own business. And even if the subcontractor did not have workers' compensation coverage, an equally solid case could be made that this was a truly independent contractor and there would be no need to charge for him as an "uninsured subcontractor."
>
> However, the story goes further. In this scenario, the subcontractor could not do the job by himself and called a friend to help him out, who was also hired as a subcontractor. Unlike the first contractor, this friend did not have his own liability insurance, did not have his own tools and equipment, did not bid himself out to work for others, and did not even have his own phone number in the phone book; all necessary items to be considered a legitimate business.

We will refer to the friend as the "sub-sub": the subcontractor to the subcontractor. The sub-sub overreached while painting causing the ladder to tip over. The sub-sub fell and severely injured both legs and lower back. The ladder also broke a window that was covered to prevent overspray from going on it, and also damaged the siding. While falling, the spray gun in the sub-sub's hand continued to paint portions of the house not intended to be painted, and paint also ended up on the grass and shrubs. In addition, the ladder landed on a five-gallon can of thinner that leaked and soaked into the ground. From all of this, the remodeling contractor ended up receiving citations from both OSHA and the DEP. A liability perfect storm.

The sub-sub contended that he was injured while under the control of the subcontractor and filed a workers' compensation claim against the subcontractor. It turns out, since the project was delayed by just over five weeks, the subcontractor's workers' compensation policy shown on the certificate expired and the renewal policy lapsed for non-payment after the initial certificate was issued. This is especially important to note as certificate holders, even those that are given additional insured status, are no longer required to be notified when a policy is cancelled. To be even clearer, no certificate of workers' compensation insurance was requested for the workers' compensation renewal as the home remodeler did not set a follow-up as the job was to have been completed before the policy expired.

When the sub-sub found out that the subcontractor did not have workers' compensation coverage, he proceeded to then file for a claim against the home remodeler. The remodeler's insurance company, rightfully so, denied the claim stating that he was hired by the subcontractor, not by the remodeler, and that remodeler's contract signed by the subcontractor actually stated that the subcontractor could not further subcontract out any work without prior written authorization. Permission to do so was not granted.

The first court agreed with the remodeler's insurance company, that it was the responsibility of the subcontractor. However, when the injured party appealed, the appellate court basically said, "We feel sorry for this injured person. You have workers' compensation, home remodeler, so you are now responsible for this person's injuries."

Therefore, the home remodeler's workers' compensation insurance company was forced to begin to pay the claim, and to their credit has continued to fight this. At the time of the printing of this book, it appears that this case will actually end up before their State Supreme Court.

The interesting thing is that this home remodeler did not even want or understand why he needed to buy workers' compensation. He did so because it was highly recommended by his agent.

The subcontractor's insurance company denied to pay for the damage to the window, siding and unintentionally painted area due to those being in the "care, custody or control" (an exclusion in the general liability policy) of the subcontractor. The insurance company also denied to pay for the leaking of the paint thinner into the ground as there was a "total pollution exclusion" on the subcontractor's policy, and also denied payment for the OSHA and DEP citations. The only item they agreed to pay was the damage to the bush.

Given this situation, I hope you now see this is a terrific example of why insurance companies charge for subcontractors. In fact, many of the state rating organizations will not even intervene in terms of an argument between a business and their insurance company over whether a subcontractor should be considered uninsured and charged for or not. Therefore, pretty much all insurance companies are charging for uninsured subcontractors.

You can also see from this example that you need to protect yourself beyond just receiving a certificate of insurance. The solution revolves around making sure you have proper contractual risk transfer mechanisms in place.

33 First, you must have a contract with all subcontractors, and that contract must contain all the normal terms and conditions: the where, what, how and how much relating to the job. No exceptions. The contract should include a hold harmless and indemnification agreement clause in it. However, given most court's rulings basically throw out contracts where you attempt to pass your sole negligence to another party, our recommendation is for you to have a mutual hold harmless and indemnification agreement clause in the contract.

(Now for my little legal disclaimer, as I am not an attorney, I cannot provide legal advice nor should you use the information verbatim in a contract. I am just conveying what is considered "best practices" in terms of what a risk manager would look for in a contractual risk transfer. Ultimately, you must run each agreement past your attorney, who would know the laws of your state, and is the appropriate person to create the final legal document that you should use.)

Second, you need to be named as Additional Insured. However, please understand that there are two types of Additional Insureds. Just because a certificate of insurance has an "X" in the "Additional Insured" box does not necessarily mean what you think.

The "standard" Additional Insured provided by insurance companies will apply while the subcontractor is working for you. If you hire an electrician to wire a house and, in the course of wiring the house, he causes damage or injuries to somebody, you would be able to invoke Additional Insured status. However, once that electrician leaves the premises, you no longer have that status. Two months later when the house burns down due to faulty wiring, you would not be able to call upon the "Additional Insured" status in their policy.

The second type of Additional Insured provides Additional Insured status including Completed Operations. Some of the insurance companies want to see specifically the wording of CG-2010 11/1985 version or its equivalent. My suggestion is that you should always get a copy of the Additional Insured endorsements from your subcontractor to verify you are actually receiving what you are requesting. In addition, on the certificate of insurance, it should clearly state that it includes completed operations so if that fire occurs two months later, you are able to invoke the electrician's policy and avoid dealing with your own.

We have also seen the Additional Insured status requested on workers' compensation coverage, which is not possible. Therefore some Risk Managers request the Alternative Employer Endorsement as a way to receive Additional Insured status. The problem with asking for the Alternative Employer Endorsement is that it is something they would not receive.

The Alternative Employer Endorsement is applicable when you have two companies that are, in essence, dual-employer of an individual employee. The most common use of this endorsement would be by a staffing business who provides their own employees to work for others but the employees remain on the payroll of the staffing business and therefore the staffing business' workers' compensation coverage. For example, there will most likely be some confusion as to whose employee it is when the staffing employee is injured under the direction of the employer that hired the staffing business. In this case, the staffing business should provide proof of coverage and name the employer they are providing employees to as an Alternative Employer. By the staffing business providing Alternative Employer status to the customer, the customer is protected should the staffing employee be injured and try to seek coverage from the customer and not the staffing business.

Another example would be a franchisee to franchisor relationship. A moving and storage business, such as Allied Van Lines or Mayflower Van Lines, is an example of this type of relationship. When the franchisee's employee driver goes long distance and crosses state lines, the responsibility for operating and insuring the liability of the truck transfers from the franchisee to the franchisor. Therefore, it is conceivable that the employee who is involved in an incident might try to sue the franchisor as well.

Many Risk Managers are misapplying the Alternative Employer endorsement. But if you do have a relationship where you are a franchisor who is requesting or requiring organizations to trade under your name, you do need to be named as an alternative employer to protect you from what your franchisers are doing. Getting back to the remodeler, having the Alternative Employer's endorsement naming the franchisor of the remodeler on it would have protected the franchisor when the injured sub-sub sued them as well.

In addition, on the Certificate of Insurance and the Additional Insured, you want to have a Waiver of Subrogation on your policy not just for workers' compensation, but for all liability coverages. This way, should you cause one of your subcontractors to have an injured employee or sustain property damage, his insurance company cannot come back after your insurance company in terms of subrogation and ultimately make you pay. This way, if there is something wrong with their employee or property, they take care of it themselves.

Wording on a Certificate of Insurance is tricky. The biggest issue is that the old certificate system used to say the agent would "endeavor to" provide notice of cancellation, but not obligated to. They just needed to try. The new certificates state that the insurance company is only obligated to notify those required under the terms and conditions of the policy. In other words, your subcontractor will be the only one notified if a policy is cancelled.

To protect yourself, you should request to be specifically added by endorsement to the subcontractor's policy under a version of a Named Direct Notice of Cancellation endorsement. Requesting 30-days notice is reasonable and most insurance companies are able to provide this endorsement, but are unlikely to offer a longer period of notification. This way the insurance company is contractually obligated to give you direct notice of cancellation.

Here are several other suggestions. On the general liability of your subcontractors, check to make sure that their General Aggregate and Completed Operations Aggregate applies on a per project, per location basis. This way the coverage for that job is the full limit of the policy and will not be eroded by or reduced by a claim that occurred at a different job site under a different contract.

You also want to make sure that the general liability of your subcontractor applies on Primary and Non-Contributory basis. This way, your subcontractor's general liability insurance policy responds first and would need to be exhausted before your policy needs to step in to protect you further.

You want to make sure that they are responsible for their own OSHA fines or regulatory fines from things like pollution as well as any kind of OSHA fines or regulatory action against you should they do something to cause you to be fined.

In addition, if the subcontractor is using chemicals of any kind, you would want proof of pollution liability coverage.

I live by the covenant to only have our clients ask for what their subcontractors can give us. I suggest you do the same. Many times I have seen Risk Managers ask for things which no insurance company will offer, or even if the subcontractor could obtain it, what was asked for would cost a huge amount of money and make it cost prohibitive.

There is one other thing you may want to pay attention to. You also need to determine what minimum liability limits are required by your insurance company so they will not charge for an "underinsured" subcontractor. Your insurance company, or its auditor, may want to see limits on the subcontractor's certificate that at least match the coverage limits you have on your policies, while others may allow you to have certificates showing lower limits of liability.

It is very important to get your risk transfer processes in place; to have solid agreements with every contractor; and to get certificates and renewal certificates from every subcontractor. Those certificates must list the terms and conditions you are looking for and, more importantly, you should request and review the copies of the endorsements providing you Additional Insured status.

Contractor and subcontractor relationships can be complicated insurance transactions with octopus like tentacles. Pay close attention. Consult your attorney as often as necessary. And do not get into a situation where the subcontractor complexities eat up all your profit.

We are OSHA compliant, so why do I have to pay for an injury to an employee that does something stupid?

You could probably make a pretty good "Top 10" list for David Letterman from what your employees have done in the past, so it is no surprise when I say some of the things employees do bring both smiles and frustration to employers. As you know, the main reason you have to pay for an injury when an employee "does something stupid" is because workers' compensation is "no-fault." No matter what happens, short of an employee being involved in horseplay or being able to prove an employee intentionally injured themselves or is faking it, all injuries are pretty much covered by workers' compensation.

Let us give OSHA credit, as they have done a great job over the years of reducing injuries and creating safer work environments. However, the focus has mainly been on the physical conditions and making sure required training is done. One thing is for certain, being OSHA compliant does not mean you are a safe business, and it does not mean the employees will understand and follow your training.

34 Most training done by companies is necessary and good, but often times it gets lumped in amongst other trainings, or it takes such a long period of time that it gets to the point where the employee's eyes glaze over and they begin to lose focus. For example, I met with an executive of a roofing contractor who said they are a safe business and provide ongoing training to their employees. But when you dig into their safety program, it consists of training from a "safety" business that comes in every year and conducts the required training – all in one very, *very* long day. Yet many employers cannot understand why they pay so much for insurance and cannot get out of the Assigned Risk Pool. They argue that the insurance companies are way too picky when they do an inspection. However, it is often insurance companies who cite unsafe work environments and poor training as the reason not to provide a quote.

There are employers who tell me everything that occurred was an accident and no one could prevent it from happening. However, my years of experience tell me that the number of actual accidents is few and far between. These employers are making excuses for their poor practices. Case in point, DuPont conducted a study of over 40,000 injuries. They broke their findings into three categories of injury causes: an unsafe condition or environment, an unsafe employee action, or an accident when no cause could be determined. Well, over 80% of all injuries come from – surprise – unsafe employee actions.

Unsafe conditions attributed to 19% of the injuries, and accidents were less than 1% of all injuries.

So I contend the focus on OSHA compliance and conducting safety training is good, but it is not attacking the heart of why most injuries occur. In too many injuries an employee says they tripped over this or fell over that, or were struck by this. But many times it is because an employee ignored the current situation and did not correct something that became an unsafe condition or environment, or the employer and employees ignored general housekeeping. Based on this, if employees eliminated unsafe conditions that they themselves may have created, you could safely assume that over 90%, or possibly all 99% (leaving only the 1% that are "true" accidents), of all injuries preventable. Therefore, it really comes down to employee behavior.

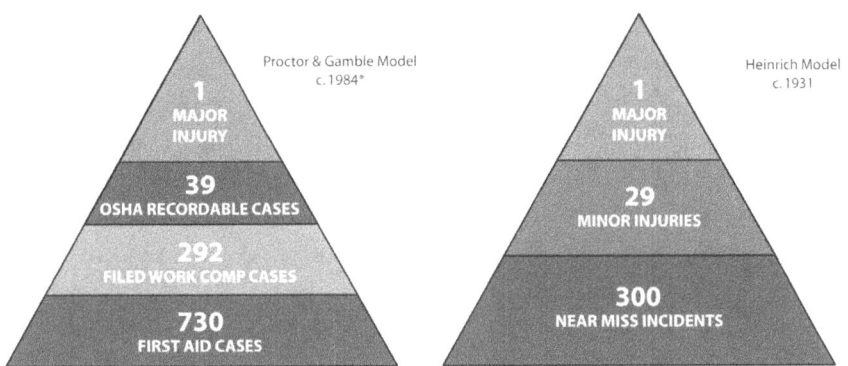

Insurance companies and loss control professionals predominately follow two models: the Heinrich model, where for every 300 near misses there creates 29 minor injuries and one major injury; or the Procter & Gamble model, where 730 first aid cases becomes 292 filed workers' compensation cases leading to 39 OSHA recordable cases, all ending with one major injury. Both of these models focus on understanding what has occurred in the past and then trying to correct that situation so, hopefully, it will not happen again. They look to engineer a solution, or try to throw some training at it so the employees will not do it again. As you can see, it is a very reactive model. It also focuses too much on the physical conditions and what has already happened, while failing to identify something new that could happen in the future.

> Very early in my career, while working with my dad in our family insurance agency, I learned the traditional safety models did not work. I remember vividly the eerie silence instead of the deafening noise usually heard when I arrived at a very large manufacturing plant. The rescue crews were bringing out an employee who had been killed repairing a machine that had just stopped working. He had turned off the circuit breaker to the machine and was replacing a drive belt inside of it when a co-worker accidentally turned the circuit back on when trying to restore power to another machine.

To this day, I still wonder exactly why the deceased employee did not take the time to install the circuit breaker lock that was in his tool bag per the manufacturer's lock-out/tag-out program he was trained on. I can only speculate that the employee did not install the circuit breaker lock as replacing the drive belt takes less than 10 minutes and he thought nothing would occur in such a short period of time.

This employee was a husband and father of two very young children. Yes, workers' compensation paid a benefit to the employee's spouse. However, what did it really do for the family? I learned at this point that even one injury can be one too many. I learned that focusing on just providing insurance was not enough. This event caused me to begin to focus more on reducing risks and affecting employee behavior, and not simply focusing on general safety and our client's insurance policies.

35 The best solution to eliminating injuries is a behavior-based safety approach. It is creating a proactive approach. It focuses on the entire employee from head to toe, building a culture, an attitude, an employee behavior that prevents instances from occurring and encourages an employee to identify those potential hazards before they occur. In other words, getting the employee to take that second or two to think, "Should I stick my hand this close to a blade? Should I put the guard back on? Should I be wearing my harness at this height? Should I be wearing my goggles before I start running this impact gun with chisel bit?"

Interestingly, Procter & Gamble has added behavior to the base of their pyramid. So, clearly behavior-based safety is the antidote to address most injuries. Business management must adopt a mindset and policy of zero injuries and that all accidents are preventable.

36 A perfect example is Alcoa's CEO, Paul O'Neill. With O'Neill about to step in as CEO in 1987, the "experts" were anticipating expansion. However, O'Neil's first act when he took over the reins of Alcoa was to overhaul their safety program. Their program was already excellent, better than the industry average. Yet he believed it could be better. He understood that safety touches every employee in the organization, top to bottom, no matter what position they are in. This is where he wanted to start to change the culture of the organization; to make it a better-performing organization. He made safety everyone's responsibility, not just the loss control people on staff. Alcoa's productivity soared and injuries were dramatically reduced. He proved safety and productivity can work in harmony and, in fact, safer practices *can* lead to better production and profit. In other words, the best and most productive way of doing something is the safest way.

The goal of behavior-based safety is to encourage every employee to think and take that one second to say, "If I do this, in this fashion, could I get hurt?" It is also about employees recognizing and speaking out about a co-worker or a supervisor who is not doing something safely or creating a situation that is becoming unsafe.

Changing the culture and implementing a robust behavior-based safety program is a marathon, not a sprint. This is not something you are going to introduce in one meeting and everything is all set. It is going to take time.

The Behavior Based Safety Model

So you ask: "What do we need to do to establish and maintain a behavior-based safety system?" Well, first, you need to define the mission and objectives of your program. Is it an organization wide strategic plan for safety? Second, you have to establish how you will measure and benchmark the behaviors of the employees and how you will gauge overall improvement. Third, you need to establish accountability for behaviors and peer review processes, and establish what all levels of the organization will be responsible for.

1 – The Mission Statement.
Senior leadership, owners and executives must be involved. This must be communicated downwards through the organization and must be delivered with a sense of the priority being safety over just productivity. Doing something safe does not mean doing something slow. But doing something too fast can certainly mean doing something unsafe. Ultimately, those that will be held accountable should be involved in setting deeper objectives so they understand what needs to be done.

2 – Benchmarking.
If you do not measure and record; you cannot determine if you are achieving improvement. Items you may want to record and benchmark might include OSHA recordables and DART rates (Days Away, Restricted Duty, or Transitional Duty), so you can compare them to other peer organizations. You should also include items such as near misses and observed unsafe actions that did not result in an injury or property damage, but were "near misses."

Keep in mind that OSHA recordables, DART and near misses should all have specific numeric goals established that reduce over time. This way you can determine the success of your program.

However, reporting by peers or supervisors of observed unsafe actions should not have specific numeric goals of being reduced over time. This may sound contradictory, but we have seen supervisors not record such incidents as they were afraid that they may be reprimanded, lose their job or a bonus, because they are not observing fewer unsafe actions. Remember, the goal is to prevent the injury, not just to make the paperwork look good. Therefore, any and all unsafe actions need reporting, even if no injuries or near misses occur, so that potential problem areas or employees can be addressed before something serious occurs.

Senior management must track and measure various components to hold the supervisors accountable. Yes, even the executives of the organization must monitor those below them to establish the supervisor is doing his or her job. Nothing undoes a safety program quicker than a supervisor who is only focused on productivity with no regard for safety.

Establish a line of communication for feedback from bottom to top. In other words, if an employee feels their supervisor is ignoring a situation that has been brought to their attention, they must feel safe that they can go above their supervisor without fear of repercussions and know who they can go to in such a circumstance.

3 – Establishing accountability and a Peer Review Process.
This starts with the owners, executives or CEO reviewing senior management, senior management reviewing supervisory, and supervisory reviewing workers. There is also a peer review process. This process includes a co-worker, maybe acting as the safety person of the day, or simply a longer tenured employee in a work group who is responsible for observing the operations of their co-workers because a supervisor may not always be present or even fully aware of all the exposures associated with doing a job.

Basically, you must be able to create a checklist of unsafe behaviors and safe behaviors for supervisors and peer observers to use. Measuring and recording is the key to this process. You will need ongoing training for observers so they can learn from each other, as well from the outside. More importantly, as your team learns these items and actions, corrections must be recorded in the training manual. This allows training of observers business-wide as well as new observers who can be trained to monitor their co-workers.

4 – Responsibility.
In establishing organizational responsibility levels, please understand it is a two-way street up and down the organization. Those below must feel free to "go up the ladder," even several rungs, to ensure you address key issues and situations. All goals and actions should be result-oriented. Everything requires reporting and measuring otherwise it ends up meaningless and without consequences. All of this will end up improving behavior.

Subsets of the levels of accountability involve personal, team, and organizational accountability:

- *Personal*
  You must empower and make each employee responsible for their own actions.

- *Team*
  There is shared accountability for the performance of a work group or team through the use of peer review.

- *Organizational*
  There is internal accountability not only laterally up and down the chain, but also externally to those who are working at a job site. The actions of other contractors could put your employees in harm's way or vice versa. From an accountability standpoint, you have the obligation to make certain you make the other contractors aware of an unsafe situation so that your

employees are not in harm's way, or correct a situation you may be causing so their employees are kept safe.

As an example of what is necessary when implementing a behavior-based safety program, we will discuss a building material dealer who had a delivery truck show up at 4:30 on a Friday afternoon delivering kitchen cabinets. All the loading dock spots were full of trucks being packed, or already packed up, for next day deliveries. The driver wanted to leave as quickly as possible. He went to the supervisor and said "Hey, I need to get going. Can you get one of your employees to help unload the truck?" The supervisor sent one of the employees out into the yard to start unloading the truck. In the course of unloading the truck and removing the cabinets, the employee fell off the back of the truck shattering his elbow.

This is not a safe environment for the employee, but the driver, supervisor and even the employee himself, were put in harm's way because they were focused on getting the truck out as quickly as possible instead of pulling the truck into the loading dock. They could have moved one of the fully loaded trucks, thereby allowing the truck to come in and get unloaded safely. Moving a loaded truck would have probably taken less than five minutes, and actually would have shortened the amount of time needed to unload the truck, in the middle of the yard, thereby getting the impatient driver home quicker. This incident should have been prevented by the supervisor saying "no" to the driver. He could have done so by simply stating they were not allowed to unload a truck out in the yard and it would only take a couple of minutes to get a truck moved so the driver could pull in.

The result is an employee who will forever have problems with his elbow, and an employer whose experience modifier increased because of the over $100,000 in medical costs associated with rebuilding and repairing the elbow. This resulted in over $130,000 in additional premium over the impact life of the claim on the modifier. Why? This occurred because the supervisor put perceived productivity ahead of safety. So the additional cost of possibly having an employee work an extra 5-10 minutes of overtime was miniscule in comparison to the additional costs associated with this injury.

So, what occurred? From an employer's standpoint, the employer correctly suspended the supervisor without pay for two weeks to reinforce to all his employees and supervisors that management will not tolerate unsafe actions or short cuts. To have your message "heard" by your employees, you must reinforce your message with consequences.

As you can see, the goal of every organization is not just to be OSHA compliant, but to actually create a safer, more productivity-oriented culture, much like Paul O'Neill did at Alcoa.

8

Why Do I Have To Pay A Claim On A Pre-Existing Injury?

This is a very common question that tends to start significant emotional, sometimes heated, responses from business leaders when they discuss a claim that "went bad" due to an employee either having a pre-existing condition or having been injured on a previous job. With a high degree of frustration, they ask questions like, "Why do I have to pay for what was somebody else's injury or a pre-existing condition?", or "How do I hire somebody who does not have a previous workers' compensation claim?", or "How can I stop hiring problematic employees?"

What I have discovered is injury and performance problems begin at hire. Ask yourself: If you were to start all over from scratch in hiring employees to fill all of the positions in your business, would you hire the same employees? Hire the same way you do today? Or would you hire differently?

In this case, you may want to begin with the end in mind. You should have the goal of hiring injury-free and productive employees, and work backwards to determine what you need to do in order to accomplish this. You can then create the steps and processes necessary to achieve this outcome.

The ideal productive and safe employee would have the skills, education, focus and attitude to be able to complete their job with high efficiency and do so safely. Productive employees are going to understand specific job duties that they are responsible for and are willing to accomplish them without constant supervision. They know how to conduct all of their required tasks, how to complete them safely and efficiently, and are willing and able to discuss with their supervisor if there are ways to improve their performance. Constant improvement is in their DNA.

These requirements may be a lot to ask for. Each position in your business may have different nuances that require adjusting what was just spelled out, but I believe you get the point.

To determine what skill and education you need to hire for a specific job, you must understand everything that the position or job entails and requires. Therefore, detailed and written job descriptions are a must. Job descriptions should comprise the following:

- Essential job functions and responsibilities
- Any non-essential functions
- Success factors and job competencies
- Physical demands and requirements
- Performance standards, including skill and education requirements.

However, do not forget to determine the attitude of the employee you want to have in that position. Do you need a self-starter, someone who is outgoing and personable, or someone that is task oriented, or perhaps a facilitator that will want to help your customers, etc.?

When you fill this position, you know exactly what your requirements are and you will be able to conduct tests to determine if a potential employee has the ability and is physically able to complete the job without getting injured. Do not forget the attitude check. You will know what skill sets are required for the job, as well as education. Hire the right skills, attitude and education, and training then becomes easier.

Finding the perfect candidate may seem impossible. However, the job description provides your blueprint for hiring, and then you can build that employee by filling any gaps. So hire first for the attitude (this is the best way to avoid problematic and drama-creating employees), then the physical requirements of the job, and then determine if the employee has the potential and desire to be trained. This way, you can train employees to achieve the required skills.

Attitude Requirements
Attitude could, and most likely should, be the most important requirement. Too often I see employers hire for skill first, but if the employee has a bad attitude they end up creating significant issues and drama within your organization. These employees also tend to become claim problems in the future. If you must have certain skills, look at all candidates that have something close to your minimum skill needs. Hire them based on attitude and train for any gaps.

To recap the job requirements: attitude; tasks, education and skills to accomplish the job; and physical requirement. Now that you have these defined, you can then determine and test your candidates to select the best person for your organization.

There are a multitude of personality, or attitude, testing programs available. Some give you the ability to conduct personality tests on current employees so you can determine what personality type your best employees at different positions may be. This will then give you some insight as to what personality type may be best suited for a certain position.

Some of the better testing systems will allow you to test your whole organization and give you a baseline of your overall culture. This allows you to better choose personalities to fit within your organization.

Most offer a nominal paid subscription program so you can test as many candidates as you want. So, in other words, test all candidates and do not just rely on your gut feelings. Many candidates can give you a great first impression that may be masking issues that will crop up later. These tests are designed to uncover those issues.

Education Requirements
It is important to verify your applicant's education and degree from the university, college, trade school, or online school that they graduated from. Verifying their degree through an education background check helps you validate their resume or application. This is necessary because it is possible for a person to embellish their resume. I have seen people actually change their degree to what they perceive to be a better fit for the job, or state that they completed their degree when they either did not complete it or were in the midst of completing it.

Skill Requirements

You must skill test at your facility or jobsite. Request your applicant to complete tasks with the tools, equipment or machines they will work with in their position. This will give you firsthand knowledge as to how well they know what needs to be done, but also if they are conducting the job properly and safely.

Just because they worked as a machinist for three years does not mean they really understand how to operate your equipment. You may want to see if they are capable of performing the functions on a test part in your facility. If you are in the construction world, are they able to discuss with you what specific steps they would have to accomplish to complete the task, or the necessary steps to operate equipment safely?

You have a vast choice of companies that provide online testing for technology or computer intensive positions. You want to make certain that any tests performed are done in your presence. When an applicant takes a test at home, at times they are not taken by the actual candidate, but by one who is more skilled than the prospective employee.

If you do not test the person you are hiring, you may believe you are getting a competent person, or even a "superstar," and you actually hired someone who may need significant training and education to complete the tasks of the job. Not knowing you have hired an undertrained employee, and not training to fill skills and education gaps, will most likely lead to you having a "poor performer" or "problematic" employee. This perception develops because it takes the employee much longer to complete tasks as compared to others. More importantly, they may miss critical deadlines, respond slowly, and upset customers.

Physical Requirements

Due to HIPPA (Health Insurance Portability and Accountability Act), only a doctor can ask a prospective employee about specific medical conditions. Therefore, it is best to work with medical professionals when screening prospective employees. The doctor can determine whether or not the candidate can physically complete the required tasks of the job, or if they need accommodations to do so. The accommodations are important because it addresses the Americans with Disabilities Act, and whether you are able to accommodate a restriction or not due to the physical requirements of a specific job.

As you can see, it is very important that you determine and write out in detail your specific physical requirements in the job description. If you cannot accurately determine the specific physical requirements of the job, reach out to your local physical therapist. They can come to your facility or job site, observe the jobs, go through the motions required, and determine the actual pounds needed to be lifted, the range of motions needed, etc.

Once you have spelled out the specific requirements, conduct a post-offer, pre-employment physical, including a functional capacity screening. Many physical therapists will gladly assist in establishing the physical requirements of the job for you at no fee.

You may then use them to conduct your prospective employee's physical tests to best determine if they can do the essential functions of the job. Testing, if you decide to use it, must be performed for all potential candidates for the job. For example, if you use physical tests for applicants for a carpenter's position, all applicants must be tested. You cannot limit testing to only those candidates you believe pose a risk. You will have to pay the physical therapists to conduct the screening tests, but the tests are nominal compared to how much an injury from a "pre-existing condition" can cause you in increased workers' compensation premiums.

You may also want to have a business doctor, ideally an occupational medicine doctor, conduct the employee physicals. By establishing a "go to" doctor who has seen and understands your business and knows what the various jobs requirements are, you can be certain the doctor is watching out for your business and is less likely to "approve" a person that physically cannot perform the job even with an accommodation. This would be the same doctor you want to send injured employees to in order to make certain you have a doctor that will help you bring the employee back to work as quickly as possible.

If the job requires the employee to routinely lift 50-pound bags, they should be able to do this without pre-existing conditions. A doctor can look at the applicant for scars on the back, knees, elbows, shoulders, etc. ask questions to determine if a prior medical condition would affect the applicant's ability to do the job. A doctor's office may be able to simulate minor lifting, but the physical therapist can actually put the prospective employee through a much more diverse series of tests. They can determine if the prospective employee is straining to lift the sack, is favoring a leg, or has some other reason they are not able to complete the physical requirements of the job. A doctor may also be able to describe any accommodation necessary to allow the prospective employee to complete the job. The accommodation can then be reviewed for reasonableness.

Another benefit of conducting the pre-employment functional capacity testing is you may have an employee who can do the job, but only has a 90% range of motion in their shoulder. If in the future the employee injures that shoulder, workers' compensation would normally pay benefits to an injured employee's shoulder recovered to 100%, or compensate them if recovery fell short of 100%. By having the pre-employment testing done and recorded, you have documentation the employee had only 90% use of the shoulder and therefore a full recovery is to only 90%, and not 100%. This will save you considerable amounts of future premium from the additional claim costs.

Keep in mind, however, that rejecting an applicant because the applicant has prior injuries, or needs a reasonable accommodation, can result in a discrimination lawsuit. Testing should be done to confirm whether the applicant can perform the essential functions of a job with or without reasonable accommodation. Testing should never be used to eliminate a candidate based on the belief that the prospective employee represents a greater workers' compensation risk.

Application, Interview and Pre-Employment Testing
You are ready to set up your application and interview process now that you know who you need to hire, and what and how you will test for it.

You can conduct the normal reference checks before you offer someone a job. However, before you are able to do any background checks, education and employment verifications, credit check, personality and skills testing, medical, drug or physical testing, you must make a conditional offer of employment to the candidate. This written offer would be contingent upon the outcomes of the tests that you are going to have them undergo, such as the drug or physical tests, and any consumer reports you are going to review.

For you to be able to conduct any tests and screenings, including reference checks or employment and education verifications, you must have the prospective employee's written authorization. The application or application packet must spell out to the candidate that by signing the release they authorize you to conduct medical and drug testing; obtain employment information, background information such as motor vehicle reports, credit reports, criminal background checks, education, licenses, and basically anything else necessary for that job to be properly done. Authorizations should be separate from the application to ensure that the applicant knowingly allows the searches to be conducted. Medical testing, including drug testing, authorizations must be HIPAA compliant and should not be part of the consumer report or criminal background check authorization.

The human resource attorney for East Coast Risk Management, an organization that I have frequently worked jointly with, offered an additional or alternative method of assessing a candidate's propensity for risk assumption or conversely aversion that is based in psychological reasoning. She stated, "It is my opinion that a motor vehicle report's purpose is two-fold; (1) Ensuring a candidate has the ability to legally operate a motor vehicle and that his/her driving record is acceptable for insurance purposes and (2) to highlight or indicate a candidate's potential for performing intentionally negligent and reckless acts. In my experience, a candidate who has several moving violations and/or traffic citations or perhaps multiple violations/citations for the same or similar act are generally a higher risk employee for improper employment acts and/or workplace accidents and injuries including vehicle operation regardless of vehicle ownership." Further she states, "This theory is applicable to all levels of employment or job categories in any industry and to all employers alike."

Once you have described this to the candidate in the application, and provided them with the detailed job description with essential functions and physical requirements of the job, you may legally ask the employee if they are able to perform all essential tasks described and necessary to perform the job duties. You cannot ask if they have a specific medical condition that would prevent them from doing the job.

You are simply asking if they are able to do the job as outlined. You could even, if available and a requirement of this job, ask them to demonstrate how they would lift that 50-pound sack, by actually lifting it, or by lifting it with a reasonable accommodation. Therefore, you would be able to see, if they have proper lifting techniques. Are they able to lift it at all? These are fair assessments. As long as it is material to the job, is in the written job description, and you do this for all applicants, you are not discriminating. You cannot decide whether or not they are medically able to do the job. This would be up to the doctor.

Have your interview questions lined up so you can achieve all the tasks necessary to complete during the interview process. Do not "wing it." Some of the best questions are asking how someone would respond to real world examples of situations your employees experienced in the past. This can give you some insight as to how they would respond and what their skill sets may actually be.

You want everybody who is hired by your organization to go through this entire process. You cannot take shortcuts. You cannot discriminate. Everyone must go through the same process. You may also want to conduct personality or education testing. All testing, however, must be job-related.

During the interview process, you want to introduce what your corporate culture is, especially in terms of safety, work ethic, personal responsibility, etc. This lays the ground work to clearer expectations that will be spelled out when they go through your initial orientation.

<u>Business Culture, Safety and Orientation</u>
Begin by introducing this employee through an orientation program. This orientation should not just be about the history of your business; it should be much more.

43 Indoctrinate your employee into your safety culture immediately. Safety begins at hire, so your orientation also needs to start with and continually emphasize safety. OSHA does require you provide certain training to a new employee before they actually start, such as hazard communication; but this process goes beyond this. Your new employee must understand the culture of your organization so they will do their job safely, not just productively. They need to understand that you have a "zero-injury culture," that no job is important enough to lose life or limb, and that accidents do not just happen. The orientation needs to convey that the employee is responsible for themselves and their team, in terms of making sure they are working safely, and that everyone else is working in a safe environment.

I contend that immediately after the required initial employment paperwork, such as completing the Employment Eligibility Verification Form I-9, that you should conduct the new employee's safety orientation. Your employees need to go through appropriate safety training before they even set foot on the job. This will elevate the goal of working efficiently and safely to being the main priority.

Many times, we see employers make the mistake of waiting for the next safety meeting, or the next safety training session. This can be a month, two months, even six months away, depending on how often they go through this process.

The orientation should also emphasize the culture of your organization, the employee's expectations, and what you expect them to do and how to do it. Educate them on who to report to, what should be the chain of command, what should they be striving for and achieving, and how often you will conduct performance reviews with the employee. It should also spell out the process of reporting issues they identify.

The culture of safety should be identified in your employee handbook, and supported by the employee safety manual and their safety training.

When either hiring or orienting your employee to your business, describe to them what their career ladder path could look like. What would be necessary for them to achieve or learn or understand to move up in the organization?

Keep in mind, when you move somebody up to a new management position, many employers make the mistake of taking a good employee, or their best employee, in a certain position and promoting them to manager. When you promote, you must also view that position change similar to hiring a new employee. Confirm they are adequately trained, educated and oriented to that position. Many managers fail because they were great at what they did, but they are poor leaders or managers. They could be too heavy-handed, too light-handed, fail to provide adequate feedback to the employee on how they are performing their job, or whatever the case may be.

The last thing you want to do is hire from within and fail to train and orient the employee to their new position. This will also lead to a problematic employee and potentially problematic employees who work underneath that supervisor.

Post Orientation
Would you be surprised that there are a higher percentage of new employees injured in the first six months compared to those working in the position longer than six months? Probably no surprise here.

After you conduct your orientation, it is critical to train the employee for any skill gap they have that relates to their job. Many employers make the mistake of providing "on-the-job training", or letting the employee learn as they go, without a clear process of delivering the training, and measuring the employee's progress.

The quicker you close the employee's skill gap, the quicker they will be safe and productive for you.

Also, when you start a new employee in their position, or move an employee to a new position, train them for that job. Rather than showing them once or twice how to do something, and then leaving them on their own, you need to have a mentoring program.

A mentoring program is where a more experienced employee, one that does things the proper way, is able to monitor and make sure the new employee:

1. Conducts their tasks properly and safely,
2. Does not slip into any bad habits that will be more difficult to break later on,
3. Does not have any skill gaps that need to be addressed.

It is important that the mentor:

1. Will work with the new employee for a period of time,
2. Is responsible for monitoring and making sure the employee knows what they are doing,
3. Will assess if the employee is conducting the job safely and correctly,
4. Acts as a sounding board for the employee to ask questions as they start to learn their position.

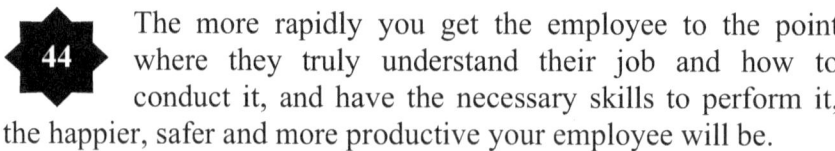

The more rapidly you get the employee to the point where they truly understand their job and how to conduct it, and have the necessary skills to perform it, the happier, safer and more productive your employee will be.

After you reach this point, be sure to provide periodic assessments and consistent reviews of their performance. On an ongoing basis, you should identify not only the areas where you can help them improve, but also commend them for the good things they accomplish. Also, look for feedback on how they feel they or the business can improve.

You would be amazed how often your own employees will be able to identify better, safer and more productive ways to accomplish the same task, or have ideas on how the business can grow as a whole.

How Do I Choose the Best Agent and Insurance Company to Insure My Business?

As I mentioned in the first chapter, many executives, when becoming frustrated with their workers' compensation, feel that they need to shop their insurance to find relief. What I find even more interesting is that I have yet to find an executive who does not feel just as frustrated by the insurance shopping process.

Face it, somewhere around 90 to 120 days prior to your renewal, the phone calls start. Every agent tells you how great a program they have and how they can save you money. They come in, try to get your policies, your loss runs, and say, "Oh, we are going to do a great job for you. We have great insurance company relationships, and we provide great service." In essence, it makes it very difficult for executives to determine if they really do have the right agent.

I contend that most employers spend less time hiring their agent than they do hiring an employee. More importantly, their agent is more likely than an employee to put them out of business.

Why do executives feel this way? I believe it starts with the traditional process of shopping the insurance. In the traditional model the agent is in a hurry to sell you a policy, even though the insurance companies will not even accept an application before 90 days prior to your renewal date. They want current information when they determine if they want to quote and how much of a premium they want to insure you as a risk.

Agents and insurance companies have conveyed the process as, "This is how you buy insurance. You go out, get a few agents, and get several quotes." But there are problems with this process. The fundamental flaw with the 90-day submission and bidding process is that it is solely focused on the sale of an insurance product. It is not a thoughtful, detailed, diagnostic system focused on truly identifying and managing your risks.

90 days is not a lot of time:

- Will the agent be able to collect all of the information that they need?

- Will they be able to obtain all the supplemental applications and complete them accurately?

- Will the insurance company accept the application or not because another agent first applied?

- How well will they be able to negotiate with the insurance company?

- Is the insurance company going to be interested or not?

- Is the insurance company able to provide all the necessary coverages?

- Will the agent prepare a detailed proposal, which may or may not be in English? It might be in "insurance-ese".

- Will the agent ultimately even present you with a quote?

Many executives mistakenly believe their organization is very attractive to insurance companies because they are inundated with calls from agents offering to quote. They do not realize that they are attractive to the agents because agents receive a commission for selling you a product; the bigger the premium, the larger the commission they will make. The issue is these agents have to sell your business to the insurance companies, who may or may not have any interest in your business.

There are multiple hurdles, barriers, twists and turns standing in your way. If you are driving down a potholed filled road there is a good chance you will hit some of them. Since there is limited amount of time and effort spent in simply trying to get this whole quotation process to work, your critical risk issues may go unaddressed, uncovered, or even worse, unnoticed.

The traditional insurance shopping process is broken. Think of it this way, each of us goes through a process when we go to buy something. It involves identifying, analyzing, controlling, financing or buying, and then using and maintaining the product or service.

For example, if you are going to buy a home, you would not ask several real estate agents to show up at your office, show you printouts of several homes in your metropolitan area that fit your requirement for number of bedrooms and bathrooms, overall size of home and yard; and then sit down and look through the listing sheet and determine which one you buy based on the lowest price of the home. So why would you buy insurance this way?

To buy a home, you are going to invest time and effort in selecting the final home of your choice. You are going to start by identifying the various homes you potentially want to look at and walk through these homes and analyze all of them to determine which one best fits your needs.

But just because you choose a specific home, this does not mean you are done. You are going to figure out how to best control or mitigate any problems by having a home inspection completed to reduce the likelihood of buying a problematic home. Once you know the issues, you can deal with them before you buy, or even choose to walk away.

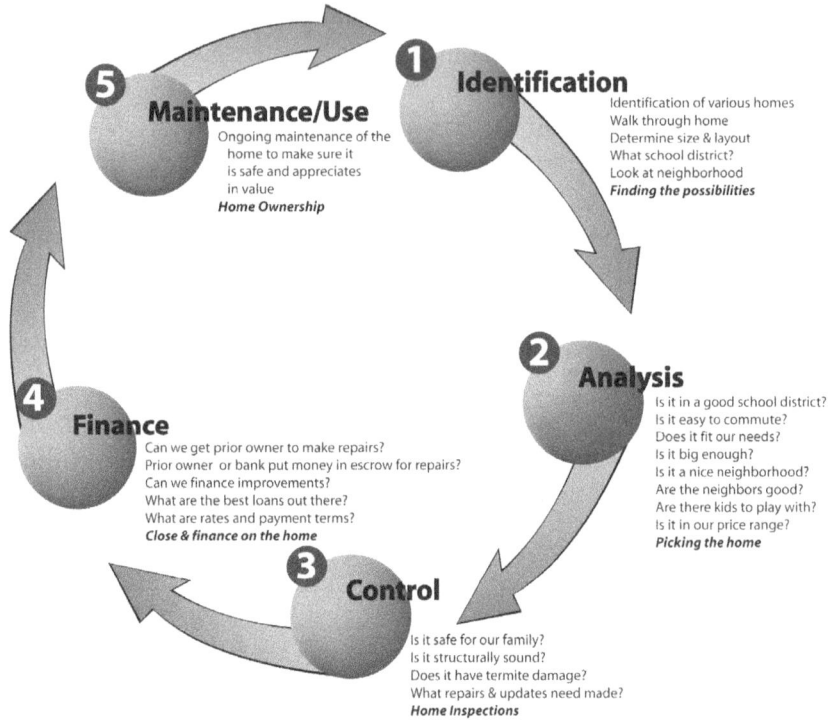

Then you are going to finance the house by searching for the best loan option. You may be prequalified for a total dollar amount you can spend, but you still want to determine which finance program is best for you. Once you decide this, you are going to close and finance the home.

Following closing and moving in, you finally get to enjoy the home and take care of the ongoing maintenance so it remains safe and maintains its value.

In comparison, the traditional insurance buying cycle lacks that process of identification, analysis, control, and administration. In the identification phase, the agent gathers copies of your policies, and maybe conducts a walkthrough and obtains loss runs. The analysis phase is spent identifying what they believe are "killer" gaps in coverage and what other policies they can sell to you. The focus of the traditional process is solely on selling you a product.

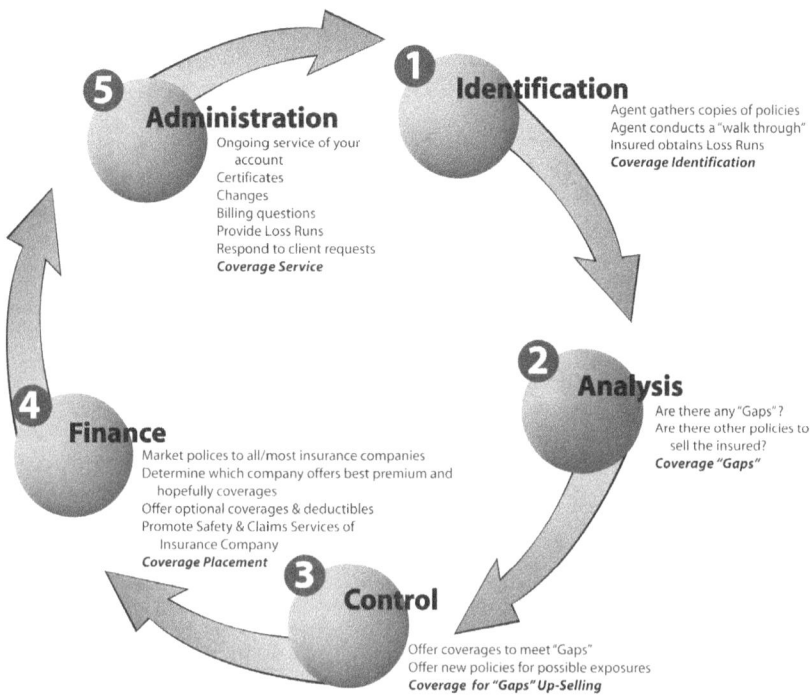

In the control step, they offer coverage to fill those gaps, or offer new policies for possible exposures. In other words, they are looking to up-sell.

In the finance step, they market your policies to all or most of the insurance companies they represent to determine which business hopefully offers the best premium and coverage, and offers options and deductibles to fill those gaps. The agents will then promote the safety and claim services of the insurance company, or they may promote somebody that wears a safety and claim service "hat" in their organization.

For the administration phase, they perform the ongoing service of your account, certificates, changes, billings, questions, provide loss runs, and respond to your questions.

As you can see, it is not really a deep identification, analysis, or control that you would have when you purchase a home. It is even worse when you want that "apples–to–apples quote." Basically, the agent goes from gathering the policies and loss runs, then slides all the way over, skipping analysis and control, to the finance phase where they go to market your policies for quotes, determine which insurance company offers the best premium, and then promises the safety and claim services of the insurance company.

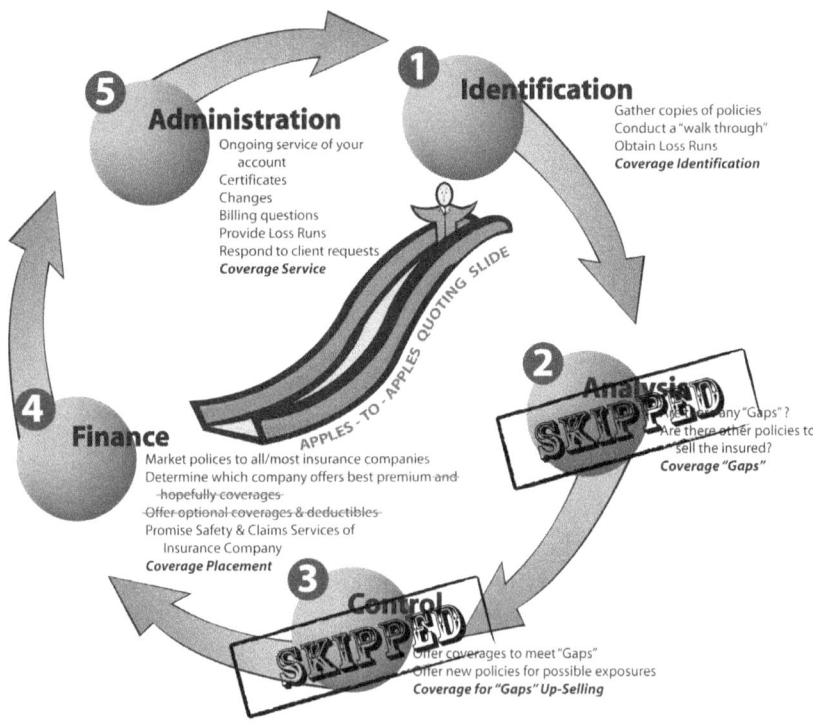

Ultimately, after going through this process most executives I talk to state that they still feel overcharged and also question if they even have the proper coverage or protection.

Take a step back. Look at what you really need to do. You must start back at the identification process and change it to identify who the agents are first. Why not interview the agents and determine and understand what their functions and capabilities are?

Ask the agent:

- What is your process of engaging with our business?
- What information do you need, and how do you gather the information you need to provide a quote?
- How do you go about this process?
- What is the experience and background of you and your team, your years of experience, who with, and doing what?

Do not put what you are looking for in your questions because remember, you are talking to a salesperson who will eagerly tell you what you want to hear. You want to find out how they believe it is best to engage with you.

Many executives tend to view salespeople as a great source of information because they see what happens inside other organizations: what works and what does not work. However, you must be sure what they do works best for you, so you can understand what expertise the agent brings.

You may want to collect resumes or bios on the salesperson and their team. Determine exactly what risk management background and training they have undertaken. One of the biggest frustrations for executives comes from the fact that many of the insurance companies and agents use the term "risk management" to mean loss control. Loss control is when a person visits you, makes a list of physical hazards they see then wants you to fix them or they will not insure you, or will insure you at a higher premium.

Risk management is much, much more than loss control. Risk management is an ongoing process of identifying risks; analyzing, measuring and prioritizing them; figuring out how best to control them; and then dealing with the risk transfer and implementation, as well as risk review and refinement. Do not confuse loss control with risk management, even if risk management is in someone's title.

Obtain testimonials and references from satisfied clients.

Talk to them and find out what processes and programs the agent will implement to help you become a better risk. What insurance companies does the agent represent? First and foremost, never get happy ears at the initial answer. Always ask more questions.

For example, I was working with a client looking to identify what agents they may want to work with. While we were sitting together interviewing prospective agents, one agent said that they had a workers' compensation claims person on staff. The owner said, "Great, that will help us."

I proceeded to ask some more questions:

Questions I asked:	Agent's Response
What process does your claims person play in the injury process?	They take the claim, and report it to the insurance company. They then follow up to make certain that the insurance company gives a claim number to the customer, and if not, gets the claim number and adjuster's name and provide it to the customer.
What do they do after the insurance company provides us with a claim number?	They constantly follow up with the adjuster as to the status of the claim.
How often do you do that?	They do that very often, probably once or twice a week.
Will you contact the business owner during this process?	Yes, they would call the owner periodically to make sure everything is going well from their perspective.

What if it is not going well?	He said that he "guesses" they would follow up with the adjuster and see if they could get the claim back on track.
Anything else?	Not really.

My question to the business owner was what was the agent doing to improve the outcome of claims? What were they doing other than basically chewing up the adjustor's time with really no benefit to you as an organization? It was clear, they were not really adding to the process. They were trying to see where everything was and that was about it.

 Included in Appendix B is a section on *Answers to Get Before You Hire a Broker*. Remember, you need to interview this prospective agent as if they were going to be your employee. Take your time. Determine who the best agent would be for you to improve you as a risk, and provide the services that you ultimately need that will lead you to lower premiums and allow the agent you chose to go to market for you. And first and foremost, do not do this during the normal 90-day time frame prior to renewal process. Start when there is no pressure to make a buying decision.

In addition to Appendix B, you will learn more in Chapter 10 about the risk management process so that you may ask more pointed questions when determining which agent you want to advise you, and ultimately represent you in the insurance marketplace.

The whole bidding and quoting process with multiple agents going to multiple companies is nothing but a headache. It frustrates employers, frustrates agents, and frustrates insurance companies. In most cases, it actually makes you look less attractive to insurance companies. Many insurance companies may pass on quoting because they believe there is a lack of control by the business in terms of this marketing or shopping process.

In most cases, you will ultimately achieve a better result by determining who would be the best agent/advisor for you in terms of helping your organization achieve your goals and representing your business, and then let them go to the entire insurance marketplace on your behalf. A good rule of thumb: seek first in order to understand before you act.

What Is The Best Way To Get The Lowest Rates?

Ultimately, what the 1,187 executives I met over the last two years wanted to know most was how to reduce their insurance rates. When speaking to executives, I always ask, "Would you agree or disagree that your premium is based on the insurance company's perception of your risk?" Without a doubt, everyone agrees.

While in college, I participated in a summer underwriting internship at an insurance company. I went through the company's commercial underwriting school and was lucky enough to work with their most senior underwriter as a mentor after the initial training. He was regarded by many of his peers as one of the best underwriters in the industry.

To this day, I vividly remember poring through the details of an account submitted by one of his agents. It was my first account. The submission was for a large construction business. Included in the submission were the industry standard applications, the insurance company's supplemental, and a rather thick packet of loss runs.

The agent had called the underwriter (and me) to discuss the account before sending it. The discussion revolved around a description of the type of work the contractor performed, how most of the losses were a "bit of bad luck" and the largest claim was a "shock loss." The agent mentioned that they were a very safe contractor. He then babbled on that he had a "great in" at the prospective client and that we had a "great opportunity" to write the insurance as the employer was very upset with his current agent and wanted to switch companies.

After going through the loss runs, my first reaction was to question whether the insurance company should even provide a quote to this contractor because of all the losses. This account was not a very good risk as they had not only a large number of claims, but a number of claims with very large amounts paid out. When I pointed this out to the underwriter, he smiled and said, "David, there are no bad risks; there is just the wrong premium. You can write any risk you want so long as you get enough premiums for the risk by pricing the risk correctly."

He then instructed me to call the agent so we could ask and understand what his prospective client has been doing to address the claims and to prevent them from reoccurring. Unfortunately, the agent did not provide enough solid details on what was being done to address the claims and risks. The underwriter informed the agent that we were not going to provide a quote unless we could get more information. The agent proceeded to press the underwriter. He believed he could still write this prospective client's business if we just provided a quote. I was a little surprised when the underwriter pulled the large electric calculator with paper tape over from the corner of his desk, looked over the loss runs, and proceeded to punch some figures into the calculator. He then said that any quote would probably be in a certain premium range and asked if we should proceed to finalize a quote. The agent responded that the range was probably 25-30% higher or more than the prospective client's current premium. The underwriter asked the agent to get him more details and he would revisit the submission. In the end, we did not receive any more details, so my first account went down as a disappointing "declination."

What I learned from my experience that summer underwriting accounts was that if you really want to drive down your insurance rates, you must improve your risk and your Risk Profile. It is a very simple concept, but it requires time, effort, and paying attention to the details.

Many business leaders believe that a workers' compensation premium quote is simply based on their payroll, the insurance company rate and their experience modifier. This is why most executives believe they need to get quotes from multiple companies, in order to find out which one has the best rate. On the surface this may appear true, but when most executives learn how the rate used for their business is determined, they are rather surprised.

An insurance company typically has several subsidiary insurance companies in their family. Each of those subsidiary companies has their own rates. I can think of one insurance company group who has 14 different subsidiaries. Those companies' rates range from the lowest filed rate in a state to the highest filed rate in that same state. This range of available rates is designed to provide the underwriter the flexibility to *choose* which of the companies and rates to use. In addition, the underwriter can apply credits or surcharges to further increase or decrease that rate. As you see, the underwriter must go through a process to decide which rate they will finally use for your quote.

In reality, the underwriter determines the premium they are looking for based on the risk of your operations. The underwriter then backs into the actual rate they will use. As you now clearly see, **your premium is derived by what the underwriter perceives to be the risk of your organization, namely your Risk Profile**. If you recall, in the first chapter I introduced my premium formula:

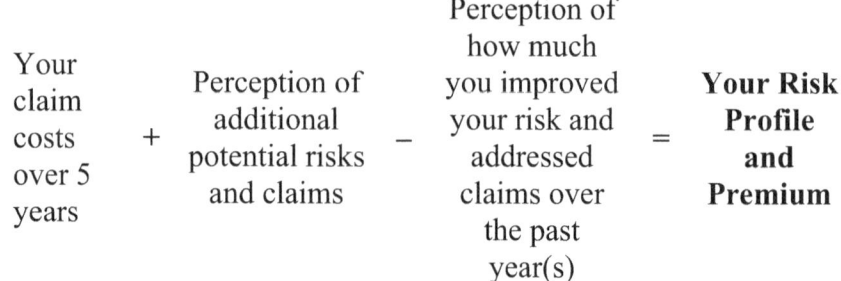

So I ask, what is your Risk Profile?

When you take time to improve your Risk Profile and reduce your risks, you will ultimately drive down your rates. Why? When you reduce your risks, you improve your safety, which will reduce the frequency and severity of injuries and accidents. Everything we are discussing revolves around what the perception of your Risk Profile is.

Going back to the previous chapter where we discussed how insurance agents come in and focus on the financing of your risk or insurance: "Can we quote you?", "Can we find holes and gaps to cover your risk and basically sell and up sell you?"

46 You need to get out of the quote and hope trap, and the poor results that come from that trap. It takes years to pass so that the claims that have already occurred and appear on your loss runs fall outside the *"Your claim costs over 5 years"* window most underwriters look at. Therefore, the quickest and best way to reduce your rates in both the short and long term is to focus on impacting the underwriter's *"Perception of how much you improved your risk and addressed claims over the past year(s)"*, and you can only do so by focusing on the entire Risk Management Process.

The Risk Management Process a five-step ongoing process that involves:

- Risk Identification,
- Risk Analysis,
- Risk Control,
- Risk Transfer and Implementation,
- Risk Review and Refinement.

Many insurance agents jump directly into step four, risk transfer and implementation, quoting your insurance and transferring that risk to an insurance company. Sadly, they do not spend the time in the risk identification phase.

Yes, agents may identify some exposures or things that could be potential claims, but their focus is to try to sell you coverage. If ultimately you are going to buy that coverage, whether it is for primary coverage or excess losses if you are self-insured, you are going to pay a premium based on your risk. If you are bidding and quoting your insurance and have not addressed your risks, you may have coverage, but you are going to pay a premium based on the perception of a higher risk than if things were put in place to control that risk. The question really is: if you control risk well enough, should you even purchase coverage for it?

As we go through the steps of the Risk Management Process, it may be easiest to understand the complete process by providing you with a general overview of how my team goes through this entire process when working with our clients. There is no wrong or right way to go through the process, just do not skimp on the process. Please make sure you go through each and every step thoroughly.

Step One: Risk Identification
During this step, you really need to dig in and identify all the risks inside your organization. Our initial Risk Management and HR Assessment is a lengthy process, but not overwhelming to our clients. It is a critical initial step because if we do not identify the

risks and gather good data, we cannot analyze them, cannot figure out how to best control them, and ultimately we cannot determine how to best deal with them through either better controls, transfer, buying insurance, etc. Let us jump ahead a little. If we decide we are going to buy insurance for this risk, we could not clearly explain to an underwriter how we improved this risk if we have first not identified it nor understand it.

When we work with our clients, it entails hours upon hours of our time gathering and analyzing data. Steps include a thorough loss analysis, looking at OSHA logs, interviewing key employees to understand and know exactly what the risks are they see in the organization. We then go through their current safety programs, their compliance, their claims reporting and management process, and their HR including hiring and orientation process. We tour and analyze the facility or jobsites. We do all of this so we can really understand your business thoroughly and completely, and be able to identify the risks associated with it.

In this stage, it is important to be open and honest with yourself or with an outsourced risk manager about your entire organization and its inner workings. If you do not identify the risks, you cannot address the risks. Trying to ignore or hide a risk is equivalent to sticking your head in the sand and hoping something bad does not happen.

Eventually insurance companies will see those risks. They will see the risks through the loss runs, or they will see the risks during a loss control inspection. Either way, they will rate you accordingly for that risk.

When we dig into your operation, we are going to be conducting a five-year loss analysis or more of your loss runs. This applies to your entire organization, including workers' compensation, general and auto liability, property, etc. We are looking for the totality of the risks that impact your business. For example, a poor fleet safety program or experiencing frequent fleet losses is important because vehicular accidents can injure your employees.

We are going to look at five years of OSHA logs (OSHA 300's and 300A's). We are going to look through your employee handbook; go through and review your safety manuals, policies and procedures. We will understand how you hire new employees and review your employment application, employment packet, how you orientate your employees, and how you conduct your safety programs and how often.

Conducting a Loss Analysis will enable us to determine the origin of employee injuries, what are the causes and types of injuries, and eventually this will enable us to know where to begin our focus on prevention. By understanding what changes or processes you implement following those injuries, we can see the holes or problems in your return-to-work programs. We will determine if you have problems with individual employees who are frequent repeaters. We may have them go through a program specifically directed at reducing the potential a repeater becoming injured again.

We conduct an Experience Modifier Analysis, where we look at your experience modifier worksheets to understand how your experience modifier was calculated and to verify if it is even correct. We can then determine what is needed to improve your injury management and return- to-work processes so we can improve your future modifier calculations. What I find interesting is, that occasionally we even find claims reported on a business' modifier that were another business'. You are being overcharged in this case.

Even a thorough Coverage Analysis, a review of your insurance policies, is important. Believe it or not, your insurance policies are a good place to understand some of your risks. The insurance company has identified certain risks they are listing, scheduling, or covering on your policy. For example, we understand how many and what type of vehicles you have, and even their use classification. These are all on your policy. Based on the size and nature of your fleet, how you control the selection of drivers and conduct fleet safety will be critical to your overall risk profile.

It is interesting that in addition to identifying risks and adding endorsements to your policy to add specific coverage for those risks, the insurance company may have also identified specific risks and added an exclusion to the policy because it is a risk they do not want to cover. I cannot even count how many times we have conducted a Coverage Analysis and seen policy exclusion endorsements relating to something material in a business' operation. In these situations, the insurance company identified a risk, determined they were uncomfortable with how the risk was being addressed, and decided to exclude coverage.

The entire goal is to eventually help better identify your risk and minimize or eliminate the issues to ultimately drive down your costs and increase your profitability over expenses. After all this information is gathered through employee interviews, through data and coverage loss assessment and analysis, we dig in and conduct a risk analysis.

In Appendix C, you will find a list of the items that typically would be looked at as part of a risk identification process. There are also checklists available online that you can use to help in the risk identification process.

Step Two: Risk Analysis
After developing a thorough understanding of your business, your industry, your corporate culture, your operating procedures, and the risks your operation faces, you are starting to move beyond insurance and towards Risk Profile improvement. In the Risk Analysis stage, we determine the potential impact of those identified risks by measuring and prioritizing them so you can determine if it makes sense to address a certain risk now or later, and eventually how much time, money and effort should be spent on dealing with a certain risk.

Risk Analysis & Prioritization Scale

		Frequency	
		Low	High
Severity	High	III	IV
	Low	I	II

You should place each risk in one of the above four category grids. The vertical is the severity of the impact of the risk; the horizontal is the likely frequency the risk may occur.

Risks in Box IV are going to have the biggest potential impact on the operation and deserve first priority. Focus on risks in Box III and II next. Those risks in Box I are a low priority.

Step Three: Risk Control
During the risk control phase, we determine which programs and processes are most effective to reduce the frequency and/or severity of that risk, and ultimately reduce the total cost of risk on the organization.

You need to take the time to understand and analyze each risk you identified. When it comes to determining how best to control the risk, it is cost versus benefit for an organization. The goal is to have controls in place for a risk, which then enables you to move that risk from Box IV to a lower risk category of either Box III or II. Eventually, you want to have programs and processes in place to move as many risks down in category from III to I, or II to I, and eventually as many of those risks to that of Box I as you can.

In a bit more detail, you would likely retain a small infrequent risk that rarely occurs and has very little consequence to it. Why pay insurance premiums to cover this small probable risk? You would not need to spend much time addressing or controlling this risk. Whereas, if that small risk occurs frequently and consistently, you would focus on determining the best way to control the risk by preventing it from occurring or reducing the frequency of the occurrence. Eventually you may want to retain that risk versus paying an insurance company to insure it.

On the other hand, if you have a risk of great significance it is obviously something you would not retain. You must purchase insurance or reinsurance for this risk. Remember, the insurance company is charging you a premium based on their perception of this risk. Therefore, dig into the risk and figure out how best to control it by reducing the potential severity and its likelihood of occurring.

Explore a spectrum of proven alternative strategies to minimize a risk. Whether it is behavior-based safety, training education, physically changing a job, transferring the risk contractually to another party or even avoiding the risk all together, the goal is to improve your Risk Profile and perception of risk, and dramatically reduce insurance costs.

Step Four: Risk Transfer and Implementation
Once you complete these steps, then it is time to implement the risk control programs and processes geared at reducing that frequency and/or severity of losses, and then conduct your risk transfer. The implementation process consists of specifically tailored programs and strategies designed to reduce those risks, which ultimately will lead to reduced insurance costs. You may not have to buy insurance through retaining the losses.

Once you implement these programs and processes, it is time to implement your negotiating advantage in the insurance marketplace. You will now be able to better leverage how you have improved your Risk Profile. It is the minus in the equation, the perception of how much you have improved your risk over the past year or years. You need to clearly and precisely convey to the insurance companies the improvements you have undertaken that will ultimately drive down the rates that they are charging.

This is also the time to look at insurance programs. You want to look at alternative financing arrangements which we will discuss in the last chapter, Chapter 11, with items such as high deductibles and other strategies.

You may realize, this is the point most insurance agents start the process and focus on trying to sell you coverage to make a commission. However, in comparison, we are in the fourth step of a process to improve your Risk Profile, which will ultimately yield better results.

Step Five: Risk Review and Refinement
At step five, we evaluate the effectiveness of your risk management programs, practices and resources under real-world conditions to make certain the programs and processes work correctly. Remember, risk management is an ongoing process. You must continue to determine if your programs are working. If not, adjust them. You also want to identify new risks, analyze and control them by implementing new programs. If you do not control your risks, you are subject to the risks controlling you.

The whole idea behind Risk Profile Improvement is to go through the entire Risk Management process cycle and continue to do so. How do you know if your insurance program is even adequate and meets your needs if you do not go through the entire Risk Profile Improvement process and the Risk Management cycle?

We talked about agent selection in Chapter 9. If your agent is not looking and asking for this information, how can you make certain this agent will understand your business and be able to respond to your needs? If they do not look at all this information, how can they truly help you to improve your organization's Risk Profile and ultimately reduce your overall insurance premiums and total cost of risk? And, if they do not look at all this information, how do you know if they even designed the right retention and insurance program for you?

I mentioned in the previous chapter why the insurance purchasing process is broken. Agents jump in at step four of a five-step program, hoping to place a policy and get a commission doing exactly what they ask, "Can we quote your insurance?" Hope and quoting are not sound risk management strategies.

Yes, they say they are going to get you the best rates, but they are doing so based on the normal information you provide. By taking the time to go through the entire cycle, you will be rewarded. You will achieve outstanding results similar to our client's results.

Another way to look at the Risk Profile Improvement Process, or the Risk Management Cycle, is to look at large companies. Large box stores, retail chains, multinational manufacturers, banks, and other nationwide companies, have an individual that only wears the Risk Management hat. They have a Risk Manager, or even CRO (Chief Risk Officer), on staff. They and their team focus 24/7/365 on identifying, managing, controlling and putting programs in place to address risk.

These large multinational companies have the same exposures as your business. They have to hire, manage, keep safe, and potentially even fire employees. They have an entire department staffed and at their disposal to help with those processes. However, most businesses do not have the resources to have a full-blown risk manager or risk officer on their payroll to work at this process. That is why it is important that somebody wears that hat for your organization, whether it is you or someone outside your firm, who wears the hat of risk officer, and helps you go through the process of identification, analysis, control, transfer and implementation and risk review and refinement.

By ultimately focusing on your risks, you will be able to drive down your premiums.

A Word of Caution!
When you are going through this process, do not bite off more than you can chew. The whole idea is to have continual small improvement; the Japanese refer to continual small improvement as Kiazen. Strive to improve your risk just half a percent, or one percent, each month.

This may not sound like a large amount, but over time, you will accomplish huge improvements and results. I have met with organizations that attempted to implement too many programs at once. The long and overwhelming employee training of too many new programs at once leads to too much confusion, and frequently leads to an increase in the injuries they were trying to prevent.

After you conduct your risk assessment and you have measured and prioritized your risks, you now want to start picking them off one at a time. Some of these risks you may be able to tackle as a group and some you may have to address individually. You just need to complete them one by one, pick away at the prioritized list of risks, and put your processes in place.

Example
I was recently referred to an organization by their CPA. He believed his client's costs were out of control when it came to their insurance. The CPA could see the impact the higher premiums had on the financials. However, he did not have a good reference to determine why the premiums were climbing faster than his client was growing. The CPA astutely saw that an analysis was necessary to determine the cause.

We met with the business owner about mid-year during their policy period. When we sat down with this business owner, we found that they would obtain quotes every year. They showed us all of the quotes they received for eight straight years. Despite receiving multiple quotes where the premiums were exponentially increasing each year, the owner believed that the insurance company they were insured by was "the best company for them." While reviewing the quotes, we quickly saw their experience modifier had been climbing the past 4 years, and the rate the insurance company was using was higher than average. Therefore, it was easy to see that their Risk Profile was deteriorating in the eyes of the insurance companies.

We conducted our Risk Management and HR Assessment to identify what risks and issues they were facing. During this assessment, we identified a number of issues and started eliminating some of the larger ones. We were able to do this very quickly as several were related. What you may find interesting was we were able to have conversations with several of the insurance companies that had quoted them in the past but were always higher in premium. We asked these insurance companies, based on their perception of risk, what programs or processes they would like to see put in place prior to renewal so that they would be able to give additional consideration when they were rating the insurance next year.

A few of the insurance companies had identified some of the same risks that we had identified. With this business, they had a very large fleet of heavy delivery trucks that were having a significant number of auto accidents. When reviewing it, we identified the business' driver selection eligibility program was lacking. The business did not qualify their drivers so there were a significant number of drivers who had poor driving records, they pulled motor vehicle reports to check to see if they had a valid license only. From a *"Perception of additional potential risks and claims"* the number of poor driving records led the underwriters to believe that the business drivers would continue having accidents. Thus the insurance companies wanted to charge them higher rates.

Working with the employer, we put in place a robust driver selection and eligibility program. We implemented and conducted employee training for a fleet safety program. The employer was even willing to put in place a relatively inexpensive vehicle monitoring system through the tracking of the business provided hands-free cell phones. This enabled the employer to know vehicles location, speed, where and how long stopped. The program even identifies if a vehicle is driving more than five miles per hour over the speed limit and also alerts the operations manager.

We instituted a defensive driving course with additional training in safe driving. Even though some satisfactory programs were in place, they really were not up to best practices.

We placed all the risks we identified, measured and prioritized, on an implementation schedule. Following conversations with the insurance companies, we reprioritized a couple of the risks to make the insurance companies more comfortable with the overall risk of the business.

By simply addressing the fleet issues first, we were able to make this business more attractive to the insurance companies and obtain quotes on their behalf to reduce their auto premium by almost $81,000. The quote they accepted was about $114,000 less than the quote the same insurance company unsuccessfully provided the prior year.

Even though we are discussing vehicles here, looking at their workers' compensation loss runs, you would see that a number of their workers' compensation claims also came from their drivers. Loading, unloading, and vehicle accidents were a big concern to the insurance companies.

By addressing the vehicle issues, we also made this business more attractive to the workers' compensation insurance company and enabled the underwriter to justify a 23% lower quote than the year before. This resulted in a bit more than $93,000 in savings over the previous year's policy. This reduction was even more important to this employer as their experience modifier was actually increasing due to their past claims history.

By installing the Risk Profile Improvement Process after identifying these risks through Risk Management and HR Assessment, we were able to reduce insurance costs in less than six months by just over $174,000.

Summarizing this example to demonstrate my premium theorem:

| Your claim costs over 5 years | + | Perception of additional potential risks and claims | − | Perception of how much you improved your risk and addressed claims over the past year(s) | = | **Your Risk Profile and Premium** |

Claim Costs – The insurance companies had paid (including reserves) $547,000 in wages and medical costs for workers' compensation injuries over five years.

Plus Potential Injury Perception – Due to past claims history and prior poor motor vehicle reports of the drivers, the underwriters were concerned that there would be a catastrophic vehicle accident leading to a $500,000, $1,000,000, or even greater injury. They were also concerned about the likelihood of a more serious back or shoulder injury from loading or unloading that would end up lasting years or even go into litigation.

Minus the Improvements – Underwriters believe in implementation of better driver screening including removal of the poor drivers; the fleet safety program, defensive driving training; the enhanced training on loading and unloading; and improving their return-to-work controls.

Equaled – An Improved Risk Profile and a 24% reduction in premium. The underwriter believed that the improvements made, more than compensated for any potential risks the underwriter perceived, enabling the underwriter to underwrite to a 35% loss ratio instead of a 25% loss ratio. The dollar amount of the losses did not change; just the perception of the risk did that led the underwriter to the comfort level enabling a premium reduction.

You must be able to not just say you made these improvements; you need to be able to tangibly show and demonstrate that the changes were made, and that the changes were meaningful.

It is obvious from this example; small changes can have a huge effect. Since then, we have installed additional programs based on the risks identified resulting in premium reduction the following year of an additional $78,000.

Focusing on all stages of the risk management cycle, identify, prioritize and mitigate risks, created a feeding frenzy in the insurance marketplace for this insurance program. You too can achieve similar results by going through the entire Risk Management Process with your organization.

So I ask, again, what is your Risk Profile?

11

Are There Better Ways To Insure My Business?

When you have your house in order and start to improve your Risk Profile, whether you are buying insurance outright for your organization or buying excess coverage if you are self-insured, it typically comes down to financing your risk and purchasing some form of insurance. There are multiple types of programs available to transfer risk to an insurance company for a premium. We will go through a number of the programs in some detail. We will summarize and provide highlights, with advantages and disadvantages. To include all the details associated with each form of insurance program would be a lengthy book by itself.

The programs range from the highest cost for you to insure your risk to the lowest cost. Ranking them in that order, starting with guaranteed cost as the most costly, then moving on to dividend programs, retrospectively-rated programs, high-deductible programs, captive programs and, finally, the lowest-cost program is typically found with self-insurance.

Cost to "Insure"	Plan
Lowest ---------- Highest	Guaranteed Cost
	Dividend
	Retrospectively Rated
	High Deductible
	Captive
	Self-Insurance

Each of these programs has pluses and minuses. Ultimately, you must make a decision based on the cost-benefit analysis for your business. You need to determine which program best suits you, your needs, your cash flow, and your financial position, so that you will pay the lowest net costs possible for your workers' compensation program.

Guaranteed Cost
A Guaranteed-Cost program is what its name signifies. You pay a certain premium based on the underwriter's perception of your risk. The only variation comes at the end of the year when the insurance company conducts its year-end premium payroll audit. There is no real risk to you as an organization, outside of retentions or deductibles per claim which are very small. The main advantage of this program is that you are able to budget exactly how much you will spend for your insurance for that year.

The reason guaranteed cost is the highest cost associated is because insurance companies are in business to make a profit for their shareholders. Therefore, they are going to determine the amount that they want to charge for the potential losses for your organization, once again, based on what the underwriter perceives as your risks. The underwriter is going to then add their expense ratio (cost of marketing acquisition, policy underwriting and service, agent commissions), the insurance company profit, and even add in for a margin of error. Typically, insurance company expense ratios are in the 25-35% range. After adding in profit and margin of error, you are looking at 35-50% of your premium being used for expenses not associated with paying any claims on your behalf.

To determine the premium of your insurance program, the insurance companies will ultimately want to calculate your policy premium in order for them to achieve an expected loss ratio of 30-50%. They will calculate the premium of an employer they perceive to be a better risk closer to an expected 50% loss ratio. Those they perceive to be more of a risk will be priced higher at an expected 30% loss ratio. To understand loss ratio, you determine your yearly average claim total using the total of all your claims for the last five years. A 50% loss ratio premium could be calculated by doubling your yearly average. A 30% loss ratio premium could be roughly calculated by tripling your yearly average.

A "hard market" or "soft market" condition influences underwriters as well. In a "hard market," where buying insurance is a little more difficult and rates are going up, pressure is on the underwriters for higher rates. The underwriters will err on the conservative side and judge a risk poorer and push more towards the 30% loss ratio, resulting in a higher premium. In a "soft market," an underwriter may be more aggressive and a little more forgiving, thus underwriting to a higher loss ratio, resulting in a lower premium. As you can see, they are taking all of your expected losses and significantly marking them up and adjusting them based on the perception of your risk.

For example, if the underwriter expected to pay out $120,000 a year in claims, depending upon their perception of your risk, and if it is a "hard" or "soft" market, they may charge you anywhere from $240,000-$400,000 for your policy.

Dividend Program

The Dividend Program is nothing more than a guarantee cost policy with a dividend potential. Based on the overall loss ratio (which is losses divided by your final premium), you may expect to receive a return of premium, typically one year to two years following the expiration of your policy. The dividend may be anywhere from no dividend on poor performance to maybe 10%, 15%, or even potentially 20% for a good or outstanding performance.

Many insurance companies like to tout their biggest potential dividend, which might be 30% or 35%. But typically, you would need zero losses ($0 paid or reserved) to attain the highest advertised dividend payout. If you have one dollar of loss, you will have some percentage other than a 0% loss ratio and you will drop down to a much lower percentage.

Interestingly enough, insurance companies do tend to charge a little extra for policies with a dividend associated with them because they know that ultimately they will have to pay out, or could pay out, a significant portion of the premium in a dividend. This way they can maintain profitability.

The exception might be a group dividend program based on, for example, an association or a specific group of businesses. The insurance company is then able to spread the risk over more policies, and therefore have a much more stable outcome from a profit standpoint. They would not necessarily need to inflate the premium of each policy to pay for the dividend.

It is important to note that the amount they choose to inflate your premium may be relatively small, so this makes it wise to ask what your premium would be with

the dividend, and what your premium would be without the dividend. This way you can compare and decide if the difference in premium is worth waiting for the potential dividend.

Retrospectively-Rated Program

The Retrospectively Rated Programs take this risk-reward proposition further. A retrospectively rated program is just what it says: after your program period is over, the insurance company will then retroactively determine your final premium. They will look backwards at what the total amount of your claims are, and then calculate your final premium based on total amount of the losses, subject to both a minimum and maximum premium.

The insurance company will calculate the final premium charge each and every year until such time the retrospective contract terminates. The retrospective contract could contain a three, four, five, six, or seven-year termination period. Most will be longer in length so that all claims close and the insurance company is confident that there is no possibility of a future claim reopening or being brought to light. On the other hand, a shorter term may seem appealing, but then your final premium will be based on total claims, including reserves that have yet to be paid, or may not ever be paid.

Your standard premium, which is the basis for the retrospectively-rated program calculation, is determined much like a guaranteed cost premium would be, which is based on the perception of your risk. The difference being, is that a retrospectively-rated premium does not include a premium size discount, and therefore, typically carries a slightly higher premium to start with as compared to a guaranteed cost policy.

The best way to understand a retrospectively-rated program is to go through an example. In this example, we will pretend your standard premium is $250,000 (line C in Diagram), and you will have had $60,000 in losses.

Retrospectively-Rated Program Diagram

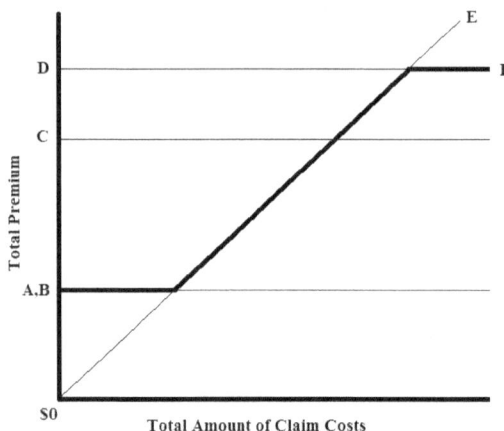

First, the insurance company will have a Basic Premium Factor (line A in Diagram), or base charge, which is their expense ratio, profit, and "reinsurance" if your losses exceed the formula's maximum rating ability. In this example, we will use 40% or $100,000 to cover their expenses and what they view as reinsurance or excess insurance should you have a horrendous loss year.

The insurance company will then add to the basic premium charge the $60,000 in losses that the insurance company paid out on your behalf, including reserves. In addition, there are usually two multipliers are that applied to those losses: Loss Conversion Factor, to pay for the costs of the claims department to adjust your claim and also allow for development of the claim as claim costs typically go up over time; and a Tax Multiplier, to cover the associated state premium taxes. Line E in the Diagram represents the final calculation of the loss portion of the premium determination.

Be aware that some insurance companies will also add a third multiplier in for IBNR (Incurred But Not yet Reported losses) to add in for the potential that a claim may be reported years later. Now keep in mind that most states have statutes of limitations on how late a claim can be reported, but this charge would be in the

Retrospectively-Rated Program contract and typically be charged well after the statute of limitations is over.

Let us use a Loss Conversion Factor of 10% (1.10) and a Tax Multiplier of 5% (1.05). In this example, if you take your losses of $60,000 and multiply them by 1.10 and then by 1.05 you come up with a claims charge of $69,300. We will not use IBNR in this example as it is not a normal charge.

As you can see, your final premium will be your claims plus surcharges, plus your base charge. However, that is a little too unstable, or too unpredictable, on both ends. So the insurance company typically will include a minimum percentage and a maximum percentage.

The insurance company will have a Minimum Premium Factor (line B in Diagram), which is normally equal to that of the Basic Premium Factor. Occasionally, I have seen some policies that have had higher minimum premium factors. Insurance companies use higher minimums when they want to use the retrospectively-rated program more as a tool to collect additional premium from a business than to reward them for being a better risk.

On the other end of the spectrum, would be a Maximum Premium Factor (line D in Diagram). This would be used to determine the most you would have to pay for a program year. It might be 120%, 125%, or even higher.

When structured properly, a retrospectively-rated program will yield a lower net premium cost to you as a business. Keep in mind the bigger reward that you want, or in other words, the lower Minimum Premium Factor, the insurance company will typically push the Maximum Premium Factor higher to have the upper amount cap. When structuring your retrospectively-rated program, you will want your Minimum Premium Factor to be low as possible, but make sure that the Maximum Premium Factor does not make the risk-reward decision too unpalatable.

So for this example, we will use a Minimum Premium Factor equal to your Basic Premium Factor of 40% (0.40), and a Maximum Premium Factor of 125% (1.25). Your Basic Premium Factor is $100,000, and your losses result in a premium charge of $69,300, thus your final calculated premium would be $169,300. So in this example, as your total calculated premium is less than your Standard Premium, you would receive a refund of $71,700 in premium. If you had $0 in losses, you would receive a refund of $150,000. However, if your claim costs exceeded $129,870, you would owe additional premium over the initial $250,000 paid in. In this example, once your total claim costs exceeded $182,247, you would hit the Maximum Premium Factor and would owe an additional $62,500 in premium. The bold line F in the Diagram represents the final premium you will pay based on the calculation of your losses.

You have to look at it as the risk and the reward of the program. You can reap the rewards of having your house in order, and achieving better results, by moving towards the alternative funding programs of retrospective, high deductible, captive, and self-insurance. By doing so, you can ultimately reduce your cost of insurance far greater than guarantee cost or dividends.

Obviously, you can see the advantage of significantly lower premiums and the flexibility of the program. The disadvantages of this program include uncertainty surrounding final premium, and the premium paid may be higher than guaranteed costs when you do not control your losses.

Unfortunately Retrospectively-Rated Programs have earned a bad reputation because insurance companies typically present retrospectively-rated programs to businesses that do not have their house in order and experience significant losses. The reason insurance companies' do this is to get the extra premium because of the losses that occur. In essence, the insurance companies use the retrospectively-rated program to provide them with additional premium. Because they simply cannot price the premium high enough to their liking, as they cannot use a high enough rate or add enough surcharges to the guaranteed cost program as they would like, they use a retrospectively-rated program to accomplish it.

At times I have seen retrospectively-rated programs with 80% to 90% (0.80-0.90) minimums and 150% to 220% (1.50-2.20) maximums. As you can see, a retrospectively rated program can be used by insurance companies as a tool to collect more premiums by creating a skewed risk-reward with the advantage to the favor of the insurance company.

On the other hand, these programs are not frequently proposed to businesses that do have their houses in order. Most insurance agents do not truly understand the retrospectively-rated program and therefore cannot explain it to an executive well enough for the executive to become comfortable with the program. Also, insurance companies do not readily offer them to business with their houses in order as the insurance company would obtain more premium from the business owner using the guaranteed cost policy.

It is very important to understand what loss levels or claim total dollars spent will equate to what premium you ultimately pay, so you can make an intelligent financial decision regarding risk-reward.

High Deductible

High deductible is that next step just before you would go into a captive or self-insure program. In this program, you accept a high deductible per claim, typically a minimum of $50,000 per claim, or higher, with the possibility of $100,000, $250,000, $300,000 or even half a million dollars per claim (See A in Diagram below). To prevent too much financial uncertainty caused by a high frequency of injuries with a high deductible program, you may also have an aggregate deductible amount (See B in Diagram below). This aggregate deductible enables you to have some maximum cost certainty. The aggregate might be two, three or four times the amount of the per claim deductible.

It is up to the underwriter and the insurance company to determine exactly what this aggregate deductible amount might be. Then it determines amounts that exceed this per claim deductible for an individual claim, or when the total of all your deductibles exceeds your aggregate maximum deductible, then the insurance company pays (see the diagram below).

High-Deductible Program Diagram

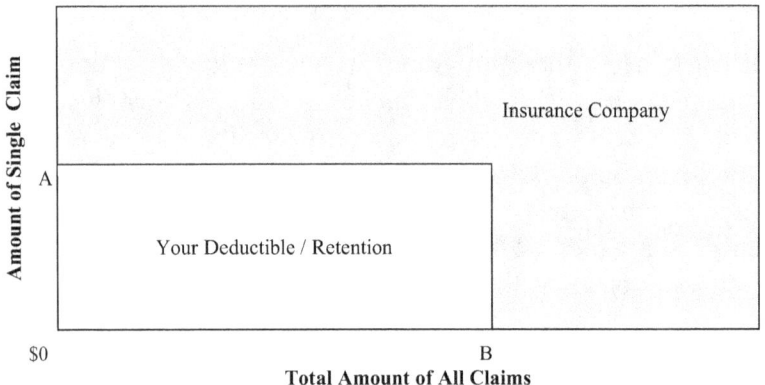

Through these high deductibles you will find yourself paying most, if not all, of your claim costs. You are purchasing excess coverage from an insurance company. You receive a substantial premium reduction through a very large credit that is applied to your policy to reduce the insurance premium portion you pay. In essence, a high deductible is not much different than self-insurance, except you do not have to deal with all of the state regulatory issues of self-insuring. All functions and services provided by the insurance company are marked up for their profit.

However, much like you saw in the retrospectively-rated program, the insurance company is going to mark up the claims for claims handling expense, development factors, taxes and possibly fees. Read your contract to understand exactly what they are adding to each claim dollar spent on your behalf, including reserves. The downside to the high-deductible program is the fact you, as an organization, can only deduct as an insurance expense against income taxes is the amount of premium that you pay, and the amount you pay for actual claims paid. You will not be able to deduct the reserves you must set aside and pay to the insurance company for potential claims.

Each insurance company decides if they want to collect the deductible payment for both paid and reserves, or if it is based on simply paid claims. You may also have to set aside either a letter of credit or supply the insurance company with a cash fund or letter of credit to collateralize and guarantee you will pay promptly any invoice for claim payments the insurance company makes on your behalf.

Captive Programs

Captives function much like high deductible; you pay for your own claims up to a point where the single claim (See A in Diagram below) and aggregate claim (See C in Diagram below) reinsurance starts to provide coverage. With a captive, you purchase a standard, guaranteed cost insurance policy, where you pay an entire premium amount that includes funding for your losses. The difference is, you then act as the reinsurer for your claims that are under the per claim and aggregate deductibles similar to a high- deductible program. You do this through the use of a captive insurance company.

A captive is its own legal entity, recognized as an insurance operation. This enables you to take a portion of your risk individually, or as part of a group, and you would earn the potential underwriting and investment income profits which normally would go to the insurance company. Now, keep in mind there still are per claim deductible and aggregate deductibles. After one or both of these deductibles have been exceeded, your excess reinsurance will pay any additional claim amount.

There are two types of captives. One is your "own" captive. If you are large enough, typically a million dollars or more in casualty premium, where you are the only business insured by that captive, you fall into that category. Casualty premiums mean premiums for liability coverage such as workers' compensation, general liability, and auto coverage. You can opt to join a group captive. Here is where you are joining similar companies in nature or companies with similar risk.

In a group captive, you may be able to enter the captive if you pay as little as $100,000 of casualty lines premiums, but most group captives require $250,000 or more for casualty lines premium. You pay your premium to the insurance company as you would with a guaranteed cost. You deduct your premium. You will still have a year-end premium audit. However, what occurs is similar to a high-deductible program. You or your group captive assumes a portion of exposure through a separately funded captive.

Much like a retrospectively-rated or high deductible, the period at which the company adjusts the losses could take three to five years to play out and for the captive year to close. It makes for a long-term investment for the dividend to be paid. But clearly it is not going to return the profits of the captive immediately, or as quickly as a dividend program.

The big advantages are premium deductibility, including the amount paid in for the loss fund, and the dividend may be taxed as a capital gains depending upon your captive structure and nature should your captive declare a dividend several years down the road.

The advantage to a group captive is you can receive a higher risk-reward similar to self-insurance when your premiums are not large enough to meet the regulatory requirements of self-insurance, plus you do not have to deal with all the regulatory issues associated with being self-insured.

In a captive, you will pay a premium for the reinsurance and an amount for operating costs. In addition, you pay in a premium for your potential losses. This is called your Initial Loss Fund, as shown in the diagram below. You also must set aside additional funds or a letter of credit to guarantee payment for the Potential Loss Fund Gap, also shown in the diagram below. The Potential

Loss Fund Gap is the total amount of premium you may have to pay if all of your losses exceed the Initial Loss Fund, and before remaining claims costs are picked up by the reinsurance company. If all goes well and you have fewer, if any, claims, you will reap the rewards of both underwriting and investment profit. However, you do have the potential to pay additional premiums when you have a bad year. In the group captive world, if the entire group has a bad year, you may need to pay into that Potential Loss Fund Gap as well.

Captive Program Diagram

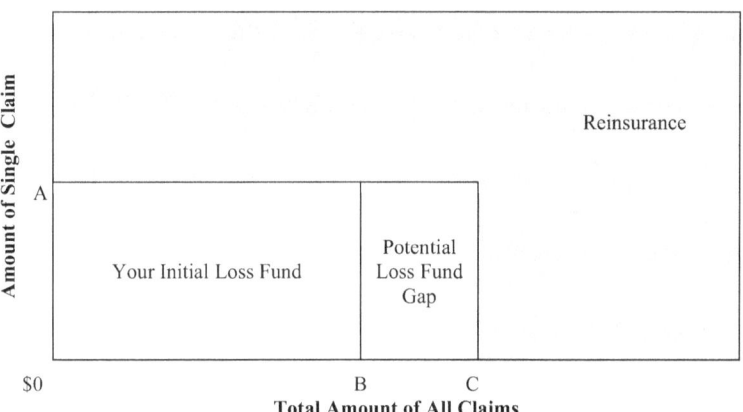

Unfortunately, I have to be a little technical when dealing with a traditional captive, versus a rent-a-captives or multi-cell captives, as there are several structures you could be involved in:

- Single Business Captive – You are the only risk in your own captive. You only need to worry about yourself.

- Multi-Cell or Rent-A-Captive – These are captives structured so there is a large, single captive company that allows multiple captives to be formed and operate inside of it. Think of these captives as being similar to a condo building. You have your own unit, but you are one of many units.

- o Traditional Multi-Cell Captive – If one of the cells, undergoes significant financial problems there may be collateral damage to the other cells in the captive, much like a fire may cause collateral damage to surrounding units.

- o Segregated Cell Multi-Cell Captive – There is a regulator barrier provided between cells. It is like having a super-firewall existing between each of the condo units. No damage is going to occur outside that segregated cell. Therefore you do not need to worry about the risk from another captive cell collapsing.

You must be absolutely certain about the state or country in which your captive is domiciled. Most captives are created outside the United States, so you must confirm it has the ability for segregated cell captives to better protect your overall investment.

The use of multi-cell captives has grown as it is more cost effective to rent a cell rather than to build your own captive. If you explore your own captive alone, or participate in a group captive, it is important to work with your captive manager to understand the structure of the captive you will participate in.

Self-Insurance

Even with self-insurance, you typically purchase excess or reinsurance coverage to protect your organization when you have a significantly large claim or a series of larger claims. Ultimately, as an organization, you should not assume unlimited risk. You normally purchase your reinsurance as your safety net so you know what your maximum annual liability (see B in Diagram) and for any one claim (See A in Diagram).

Self-Insurance Program Diagram

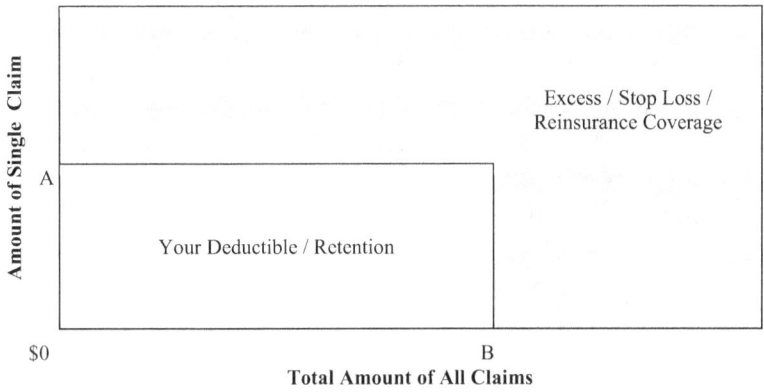

When you self-insure you must file with the state insurance department and receive approval. Most states will even tell you what reinsurance to purchase, stating the per claim and aggregate retention amounts. You must also hire a third-party administrator to legally adjudicate your claims unless you have a licensed adjuster on staff. You must also set aside monies to pay your claims and future claims, also known as reserves. You must also have your program audited by an independent auditor to evaluate and make sure you properly fund your program.

As I mentioned with high deductibles, you will be able to tax deduct your excess premium and all the fees that you pay for claims administration and actuary services, as well as the actual amount you pay for claims. However, you will not be able to deduct the amounts that you must set aside for reserves. Therefore your reserve set aside is included for income tax purposes.

However, being as you administer much more of the process, the cost structure of managing self-insured is lower than in a captive, and much lower than high deductible programs. Therefore, your overall self-insurance will traditionally lower your net cost overtime more than a captive, high deductible or guarantee cost.

Several Words of Caution

So as you can see, the more risk you take, the lower your cost of risk, i.e. your insurance cost. However, never take that huge step into the alternative funding, or any change beyond guarantee cost unless you conduct an analysis, and understand your risk-reward. You also need to understand cash flow implications and collateral requirements of each model, so that ultimately you achieve your goal of dramatically reducing your costs.

One of the things I have seen in alternative funding programs, such as retrospectively-rated, high deductible, captives, and self-insured, is many employers go into them knowing they are still going to reduce their overall cost of insurance. But their downfall may be that their house is not order. When you actually calculate and analyze their costs, they may still be paying too much. The cause of higher costs could be the frequency and/or severity of claims caused by a lack of attention to the entire risk management cycle as they are focused on other things going on in their organization.

Case in point: I met the CFO of a multi-state retail store chain at a conference in which I was a speaker. He came up to me after my session and asked why I believed that using the experience modifier could be used as a benchmark to determine how well one is managing their risks. He stated that experience modifiers do not really apply to his business, since his business was in a captive and modifiers really do not have an impact on his premium. It turned out that in each state of operation, his business suffered with surcharged experience modifiers.

I agreed with him that insurance costs will be lower in a captive than guaranteed cost coverage. I then questioned why his business, in comparison to their peers, as still having frequency or severity of claims, and therefore, paying too much out in terms of "insurance costs." He responded that he had not considered it in this light. He believed his business was getting the lowest premium using a captive versus using a guarantee-cost program. However, he did not fully realize his business was ultimately still paying too much. The business was not where it could be if its house had been in order and their claims under control.

So as I mentioned about retrospectively-rated programs, an alternative financing program can be used to mask a problem. Even though you may be in alternative funding, you need to continually analyze and benchmark your results. You must compare yourself with your peers and with other organizations, plus benchmark internally to what your experience modifier would be if you were not self-insured.

It is a continual process of benchmarking and monitoring your performance that determines whether you achieve your ultimate goal of achieving the lowest possible workers' compensation costs. Make certain problems are not being masked by your program design, thus causing you to waste significant dollars that could be better used elsewhere within your organization.

Appendices

Appendix A

PREMIUM AUDIT CHECKLIST TO CONFIRM YOU ARE NOT OVERPAYING		Yes	No	N/A
	Verify dates on the audit are the same as dates on the policy			
	Verify accurate classifications			
	Does the policy contain class codes not on the audit			
	Verify overtime (except PA & DE) and officer exemptions/limitations			
	Verify other "excluded remuneration"			
	Review Certificates of Insurance from Sub/Independent Contractors			
	Verify applicable credits, discounts, and use of correct experience mod			
	Verify all math is accurate			
	Verify deposit premium (how much was paid in)			
	Was the policy cancelled mid year			
	Is there an Anniversary Rating Date that is different from the policy's effective date			
	Does the audit add a charge for uninsured subcontractors			
	Does the audit include a charge for paid commissions			

	Is there a charge for casual labor			
	Review physical operations to see if minor facility changes allow reclassifying employees to take advantage of lower rate			

Appendix B

ANSWERS TO GET BEFORE YOU HIRE A BROKER

When asking your questions, rule number one is to relax and take your time. Remember, do not offer what answer you are looking for in the questioning. Make sure you watch their body language to see if they are comfortable, or struggling to answer. Treat this as an interview, as if you are determining whether or not you will hire this person, just like you would hire an employee.

What would be their process of engaging with your business?

What information do they need, and how would they gather the information they need to provide a quote?

How they would go about this process?

What is the experience and background of their team, their years of experience, who with, and doing what?

What specific processes or programs will you implement to help reduce our workers' compensation costs?

    If they mention Loss Control Services:

1. What services does their prevention person provide?
2. How often will we see their prevention person?
3. What credentials does their loss prevention person have?
4. How long have they been doing this?
5. Are they a dedicated injury prevention person or do they have other duties?
6. How many clients does their prevention person currently work with?

If they mention Claim Services:

1. What involvement will their claims person have with a claim?
2. What type of questions does their claims person ask to determine the severity or validity of a claim?
3. How many claims is their claims person currently handling?
4. Are they a dedicated claims person or do they have other duties?

What is your best practice to make sure our audit is accurate?

What is the best practice to make sure our experience modifier is accurate?

What is the best practice to make sure an injury is mitigated?

Does your process return injured workers in three days or less?

Who typically establishes your panel of physicians?

What criteria are used to determine who is on your panel of physicians?

How would you improve the Risk Profile of our business?

What steps or processes do you go through to do this?

Can you show testimonials, or allow us to call references, that are satisfied with their results? May we see or call them now?

Can you send us a resume or bio for each of your (broker's) team members?

Appendix C

Items Reviewed as Part of Risk Management and HR Assessment

- Tour of Facility and/or jobsites
- Interview of key employees
- 5 Years of Currently Dated Loss Runs (All Insurance Policies)
    - Description of each claim over $10,000
    - Analysis of claims by type, cause, time, from date of hire
- 5 Years Premium History
- 5 Years of Payroll History
- 4 Prior Years of OSHA 300 Logs and 300A Summaries
    - Current Year to Date 300 Log
- 3 Years of Experience Modifier Worksheets
- BLS Frequency and Severity Rates Industry Comparison
- Injury Reporting & Investigation Forms and Procedures
- Return-to-Work Manual
- List of Physicians Currently Used
- Safety Manuals/Polices & Procedures
- Employee Handbook
- Employment Applications/Packet
- New Hire Procedures
- New Hire Orientation Material and Procedures
- Insurance policies including all endorsements
- Subcontractor/Independent Contractor Agreement
- Certificates of Insurance
- SAFER reports (if you fall under DOT regulations)

Acknowledgements

I would like to thank my colleagues Mike Lukart, CSP, CWCA of East Coast Risk Management; and Bob Seltzer, CIC, CWCA and Steve Stramara, CIC, CWCA of the Seltzer Group for their collaboration in building our joint Behavior Based Safety Program. ECRM is headquartered in North Huntingdon, Pennsylvania, and services clients across the country from multiple state offices. The Seltzer Group is based in Orwigsburg, Pennsylvania.

I would like to also thank Preston Diamond, Managing Director of the Institute of WorkComp Professionals, for challenging me to compile, track and record the details and results of two years of meetings and working with business owners and executives. The Institute of WorkComp Professionals is dedicated to educating professionals in managing workers' compensation. Over the past 10 years, the Institute has helped me refine some of the programs and processes we use to reduce our client's costs.

About the Author

David R. Leng, CPCU, CIC, CBWA, CWCA, CRM

David R. Leng is Vice President and an Executive Partner of the Duncan Financial Group – he is a 25+ year veteran of the Risk Management and Insurance industry and is regarded as one of the brightest minds in the industry due to his unique *Risk Profile Improvement Process*, which identifies, controls and reduces the risk factors inherent in any business that drive costs to an organization's bottom line and hinders employee productivity. Since 2004, David has saved his clients well over $21,000,000 in premiums and overcharges.

David was awarded the *Advisor of the Year for 2008* by the Institute of WorkComp Professionals and is a frequent contributor to *Dynamic Business, Environmental Health & Safety* magazines, and has been published in several other periodicals and association newsletters.

David, who has 16 years experience specializing in Workers' Compensation, is an alumnus of Penn State where he received a Bachelor of Science in Insurance and Risk Management. His professional designations include Certified Insurance Counselor (CIC), Certified Risk Manager (CRM) and Charter Property Casualty Underwriter (CPCU), Certified Benefits & Wellness Advisor (CBWA), and he's been designated a Certified WorkComp Advisor (CWCA) by the Institute of WorkComp Professionals.

David is also Co-Founder of Keystone CompControl, the nation's largest single network of Workers' Compensation specialists, and is one of only 14 nationwide *Level-5 Advisors* of the Institute of WorkComp Professionals.

David is a frequent speaker for the Westmoreland HR Association, the National Workers' Compensation Symposium, PA Society of Public Accountants, SMC Business Councils, as well as other organizations; and was added to the faculty of the Institute of WorkComp Professionals in 2012.

David spends his leisure time boating in the summer and skiing in the winter with his wife, Lynn, and their two children, Alizabeth and Luke. David and Lynn are active members of Emmaus and Autism Speaks, organizations that help support individuals with special needs, including their son Luke, who was diagnosed with Autism at the age of 18 months.

David's hobbies include woodworking and ice hockey, as well as donating considerable time to his local high school by helping to design and build sets for their musical productions.

David can be contacted at (724) 863-3420 ext. 3329 (toll free at 888-383-3420 ext. 3329), or emailed at dleng@duncangrp.com.

A journey starts with one step!
— Lao-tzu, Chinese philosopher 604 B.C.

To help you on your journey to dramatically reduced workers' compensation costs, eliminated frustrations, and zero overcharges, we would like to provide you with tools and resources you can use to reach your destination.

Register your book today to receive your Reader Bonus!

Visit **FRUSTRATEDANDOVERCHARGED.COM/REGISTER**
to receive these *FREE* resources:

SUBSCRIPTION – receive a complimentary subscription to our monthly *WorkComp Advisory* e-Newsletter full of tips, case studies, and current events that impact workers' compensation costs.

ADMISSION – to Workshops and Webinars designed to provide you with more detailed information on the "how to" of reducing costs, and identifying and managing risks.

RESOURCES – in addition to our AuditCheck™ Program, receive resources and tools you need to take control of your workers' compensation program.

CONSULTATION – complete our discovery call questionnaire and receive a 20 minute consultation call to help you get further on your cost reduction journey or help in solving a tricky issue.

RECEIVE ALL OF THE ABOVE *FREE* RESOURCES
BY REGISTERING YOUR BOOK AT

FRUSTRATEDANDOVERCHARGED.COM/REGISTER

www.ingramcontent.com/pod-product-compliance
Lightning Source LLC
Chambersburg PA
CBHW071406210526
45465CB00001B/269